**two fish**

DISCOVERING THE GOD

OF IMMEASURABLY MORE

ADAM WALKER

Adam can be reached at the following places:

walkeradamk@gmail.com

www.twofishministries.com

Acknowledgements

This is my first attempt at writing a book. My writing will probably reflect it. I was so moved by the Holy Spirit to tell this story that I couldn't resist it any longer. In fact, I had started writing this book during the 2017-2018 school year. Life took over and I had put it down for quite a while. On a long walk one morning, during prayer time, the Father spoke to my heart, "Finish the book." I got right on it.

Anyone who has ever written a book can probably tell you how great a challenge it is and how much of an investment it takes. Although short, this book is no different. It tells an amazing story of the God of the Bible at work in the present day. I have been blessed in this life to be a part of it.

That being said, the credit is due to God in all things, all ways, and at all times. He is the One who holds the answer for our problems. He is the One who gave life so that we may have life. All glory is due to Jesus, the King who died for us, even while we were enemies. Thanks be to the Holy Spirit of God, who played a more than significant role in writing this story.

I would be remiss if I did not recognize the many people who have blessed my life and allowed me to be a part of what God was doing through us all together. I owe a special word of gratitude to Fran Fluhler, Thor Erlingson, Jeff and Lisa Burgess, Gary Jordan and all the Manna House team for believing in Jennifer and I and allowing us to be a part of their mission in Madison County. We love you guys and you have done wonders for our faith!

Thank you to all our House of the Harvest team, our board, and all the people who are a daily part of its' operation. I could never name them all. It is an honor to serve our community as a co-director of House of the Harvest and it is an honor to do that work alongside Jennifer, my wife and best friend of eleven years and counting. We have been touched by every volunteer, every donation, and every act of kindness that has made House of the Harvest what it is today. We couldn't do it without you and there is no story without you.

Thank you to Alan Moss, Brian Privett, Andy Blackston and all our family at the Light. You guys have been a great encouragement to me! Our family has been blessed by so many of you countless times over the years. I am grateful to so many who have served as mentors, been willing to come alongside of us to meet any need and have supported us through our ministry at House of the Harvest, with your children, and with our body at the Light.

I owe a special gratitude to Michael McAllister, one of my sixth-grade students at Sparkman Middle two years ago. Michael is the one who inspired the Two Fish name as we sat in class one day. Jennifer called me to ask for my help in coming up with a name for her summer feeding program at Horizon. My creative mind was at a roadblock that day. Maybe it was the Holy Spirit that inspired me to ask my class for ideas.

I also want to say a special thank you to Tony Pitsinos. Since my family found a home at the Light, you have been one of my most cherished friends and spiritual mentors. It was your words on the story of John 6 that inspired this book. I am so grateful for your desire to be available to the Spirit of God and how you have influenced the same in my life. You are my Barnabas! Thank you, brother.

I also owe a special thank you to Drew Mobley, our son, for his tireless work to help me bring this book to completion. You are always willing to give of your time, energy, and ideas. I appreciate your partnership.

I want to thank my Mom and Dad. You raised me to appreciate and respect the God of the Bible. The foundation of understanding you influenced in my life has been a blessing that I believe God has used in the lives of others. I am grateful beyond words for that influence.

And most of all, I want to thank my wife, Jennifer. You are my best friend. I am so grateful to be able to do life with you and to do ministry with you. It is my greatest blessing on this earth. You have been so patient with me for so many years and you have always been my greatest support whether coaching, teaching, driving kids home from the gym, running food pickups, studying, writing, speaking, or whatever. It doesn't matter. You support everything I do. You have always been my greatest assistant coach, cheerleader, partner, you name it. I am honored to be your husband. Thank you and I love you.

God has been faithful in bringing this book together, despite my inabilities. I am so excited to see how He uses it for His glory. It is with great humility that we pray for the message of Two Fish to go forward and increase His Kingdom.

CONTENTS

INTRODUCTION

It's one of my favorite Bible stories. Always has been. I think because of the nature of the story itself, but also because of what it teaches. It's one of those stories that just makes you love Jesus more. Yes, His power is manifest in this story. But we also get to see a picture of His compassion. His wisdom. And His grace. In fact, as I have grown older and looked at this story more deeply, I have come to see a beautiful analogy to life. And that is what this book about. Two Fish. One little boy, who gave all that he had to Jesus and saw what the King of the World was able to do with those two fish and five loaves.

How incredible would it have been to witness what happened that day? How incredible to be the young boy that handed over that small amount of food, no doubt fearing that he would not eat that day, and then watch as twelve baskets of leftovers are collected. How incredible to see the teaching moment between Jesus and Philip as Jesus asked, "Where shall we buy bread for these people to eat?" (John 6:5 NIV). Philip's response, "It would take more than half a year's wages to buy enough bread for each one to have a bite!" (John 6:7 NIV). As if to say, "Forget about the place to buy the bread, what about the money? Did you think about that?"

Yet, Jesus draws this little boy into the story. I love that about Jesus. The greatest man that ever lived. The Creator of life itself. The Savior. Messiah. King. The one, who in all His humility, says, "Let the little children come to Me," (Matthew 19:14 NIV) as if He had to convince the others that He had the time, energy, compassion, and desire to sit with the little children of the world. The grown up things could always wait, because Jesus says, "The Kingdom of Heaven belongs to such as these" (Matthew 19:14 NIV).

So, the Messiah who walked on water, healed the blind, calmed the storm, and told the lame to "pick up your mat and walk" (John 5:8 NIV), draws this little boy into this moment to be a part of a miracle. And I can envision, as Andrew shouts out, "This boy has food!"

Jesus glancing his way, calmly acknowledging him, and then inviting the young boy to Him with such humility, grace, love and acceptance.

The boy approaches in fear. In his mind, knowing what is about to transpire. He has been hungry before, and he sees it again in his very near future. Normally, he would think this man would take what he has, feed himself and maybe even a few of His closest friends and leave the boy with nothing. But for some reason, on second look, the boy gets the sense that this man is unlike anyone he has ever spoken to before. And, in such a childlike manner, he trusts Him. He can't even explain to you why. Maybe it's the softness in His eyes. Maybe the compassion that He wears on His face that invites people toward Him. Maybe the way He interacts with His followers. Maybe it's a subtle push from the Spirit of God and a whisper through the recesses of the boy's mind, "Go ahead. It's okay. I promise." If he could retell the story today, he wouldn't even be able to find the words to express what moved him forward, but in that moment of anxiety, apprehension, and fear...he stepped forward.

And I picture Jesus walking forward to meet him, dropping down to a knee, and placing one of those soon-to-be nail-pierced hands onto the boy's shoulder. And calmly asking the boy his name. And replying, "Hey, I am Jesus. Can I ask that you give what you have here for everyone? I know it doesn't seem like much, and that doesn't make a whole lot of sense, but my Father can do so much with so little. If you trust Me, there will be more than enough for everyone and you will leave here with more than you have now."

The young boy hands over the basket that carries those two small fish and those five barley loaves, somewhat reluctantly. Even Jesus' closest followers, the ones who have seen Him heal the sick and the lame, the ones who have watched the water turn to wine, are watching with doubt in their minds. Andrew commented, "How far will they go among so many?" (John 6:9 NIV). There is no doubt that the young boy is feeling hesitant.

Jesus takes the basket and replies, "Thank you, son. You will not lose your reward" (Matthew 10:42 NIV). He hugs the little boy and whispers in his ear, "Behold the power of God." He rises to his feet, takes that same hand and pats the boy on the head, messes up his hair a little, turns to address the crowd, recognizes the boy's humility, applauds his heart, gives thanks to the Father, and then begins to distribute the never-ending loaves and fish to the crowd.

Everyone watches as the loaves and the fish seem to never leave His hand. It's like He is giving it out, but the basket never empties! How the faith of those people present must have grown that day. The flashbacks they must have had to the stories that had been passed down in their families for generations about God raining manna and quail from Heaven when their ancestors were in the wilderness. Today they were able to see the glory of the Father right in front of their very eyes. And all through the gift of this little boy, who was willing to give everything that he had, although it didn't seem like very much.

Jesus stood in front of His disciples and said, "You give them something to eat" (Matthew 14:16 NIV), realizing how foolish the comment would seem to them, but in that same moment...knowing that was the very thing He was about to do. This is the One who transcends everything that we can imagine. The One who works in ways beyond our comprehension. The One who has the compassion to feed all the multitude and the power to do it with nothing. This story is recorded in all four gospels. I think because it teaches us so many lessons. It wasn't within Andrew, Philip or Peter to feed any of those people. But it didn't have to be...as long as they knew where to turn. In that moment, they would learn. Just like the moment when the storm was overtaking the boat. Just

5

like when the fear of the storm became greater than the faith to continue walking on the water.

Jesus fed the 5,000 from a place of compassion. But while being compassionate, He was also teaching His disciples dependence in the moments of uncertainty. It's so easy for us to become detached from this story. If the ones who were closest to Jesus fail to see with eyes of faith, how hard is it for us to see the world through the same lens. How hard is it for us to face feeding the 5,000 with faith and not with the same questions His disciples did? Where will the food come from? The funds? How?

The answer for Philip and Andrew was there all along. The answer for the 5,000 was there the whole time. And it still is today...even when we fail to put our trust in the power of immeasurably more. Our world teaches us to trust in ourselves, our thinking, our resources, our capabilities. Our Savior teaches us to trust in Him, His wisdom, His power, and His Father. In our culture, we have gotten away from a God who can calm the storm, feed the multitude, heal the sick, and raise the dead. Our culture has wandered in the wilderness away from the God of the Bible. We have come to know a God who is behind-the-scenes, passive, who set the world in motion and sat back and watched. Many of us have come to believe in a

God who wrote the Bible story and upon its' completion stopped being active in the world.

This story has left many of us, maybe all of us, longing for the God of the Bible. The God we see in the story of the two fish and five loaves, that is so full of compassion that He has to intervene in the lives of His children. It's as if He is there the whole time as He promises, waiting for us to recognize our need for Him and grow in our ability to trust in Him. That is the story of Two Fish. This book is about my journey of learning to experience the God who is present, compassionate, and involved. It's about coming to understand how He desires for me to just bring Him what I can bring Him every day and then trust Him to do the rest because He is the One who can use our gifts, accelerate our gifts, and multiply our gifts...all to His glory.

I pray that one day I can hear the Two Fish story from the eyes of the little boy who handed over the two fish that day. What would it be like to hear him tell that story from start to finish with all the emotions, questions, fears and insecurities? We can only imagine. But until that day, my prayer is that my Father would rewrite that story through my life, through all of our lives. I desire that we all have our own testimony of bringing just our Two Fish and experiencing what the power of God will do with it. My prayer is that through this book, you will find what God desires for you to give and you will give it freely, no matter how small it may seem, and that you will be able to see and testify to how big your God is and how many thousands He can feed through your small Two Fish. He is the God of immeasurably more. I want to know and experience more, a whole lot more.

1

Making Plans

It was the summer of 2012. I was beginning my third year teaching at Sparkman Ninth Grade Academy. I had come over from Westlawn Middle School after teaching there for one year, the year Westlawn and Stone Middle merged. Jennifer, my wife, was trying to find her way back to work. She had taken classes to renew her certification, which had expired while she was home with our son, Ty.

She had applied for a job at Discovery Middle School. That was the job she really wanted. Jennifer went to high school in that building when it was formerly Bob Jones. We knew she was going to get that job. Ty and I met her in the parking lot after her interview with flowers to celebrate. She came to the car and said, "I am not getting the job."

The principal really loved her. In fact, she told her that she would try to hire her in another position in the future. Reality was, they needed a softball coach. Jennifer is a lot of things, but a softball coach isn't one of them. I still remember that moment. I was so disappointed for her. I remember us losing our sense of direction in that moment. It's hard to be in that place where you build yourself up to an expectation that just doesn't become reality. That is a miserable feeling.

You know that feeling you have when you already have done all the planning and you already have it all figured out? You know how it's going to go. You already wrote the script. Then, something big doesn't go according to the plan. Wait, wait, wait...this can't be right. This is not supposed to be how this was going to happen. I mean, I already had this planned out. I already wrote this part. I had it so perfectly orchestrated in my mind. I was in complete control and had it all figured out. Until all that planning was wrecked...in this one moment. You can relate?

The Bible speaks of a man named Moses who had a similar experience. In fact, the best I can tell, he had several similar experiences. From the time he was a baby, God had a hand on Moses. He had plans and purposes for Moses long before Moses was even aware of God's presence in his life, before he was even born. Just like He does for you. Just like He does for every one of us.

Moses was an Israelite. Tribe of Levi. He was born into slavery in Egypt. In fact, he was born at the worst possible time for an Israelite to be born in Egypt...a male Israelite anyway. Pharaoh had ordered all the male Israelite children thrown into the Nile River because they were overpopulating the Egyptians. Pharaoh was ruthless. Power can make us that way. Even more so when it is coupled with fear.

Moses' mother protected him for three months. After three months, she couldn't hide him any longer, so she put him in a basket and hid him in the reeds on the bank of the Nile River. Moses was found by Pharaoh's daughter. In fact, she would give him the name Moses. He would eventually become the son of Pharaoh's daughter. Moses would grow up with the "treasures of Egypt" (Hebrews 11:26 NIV), as the Bible describes it, to find out he was a child of one of the Israelite slaves. How is that for "not exactly the script I had in mind?"

Before long, Moses would find himself sympathizing with his Hebrew family. Exodus 2 tells us he went and watched them at the "hard labor" (2:11 NIV) forced on them by Pharaoh. It was there that he saw an Egyptian beating one of the Hebrews. Moses killed the Egyptian and hid him in the sand. Probably not part of the script.

As Pharaoh pursued Moses to kill him, Moses would leave Egypt and go into hiding in Midian. Moses went from having all the treasures of Egypt to not knowing where he is, where he is going, or even where he will get his next drink of water...and it all happened overnight. This is definitely not according to the plan.

God was with Moses in the middle of all of it. Even when he had no idea, nothing looked right, and nowhere was home. To me, that is the most reassuring thing. God was in his story when he was a baby in the arms of Pharaoh's daughter. God was in his story when he was a prince in the wealthiest land on earth. And even though he didn't have a clue, God was in his story when he was all alone with no answers, and more questions than he had time to ask. And he had all the time in the world.

I think this is exactly what God wants you and me to hear. He is there in the good. He is there in the bad. And He is there in the worst. He is there in the crowd. He is there when loneliness is the path you walk. He is there when we can't see Him. And even when we simply are choosing not to. In fact, our state of mind never changes the fact that He is there. Didn't change it for Moses. Doesn't change it for me. And neither does it for you. He is there.

As the story continues, God came and found Moses when the time was right. Actually, Moses kind of found Him. When Moses had gotten to a place where He was available, he was able to notice what God was doing. Moses noticed that burning bush. It was there that God made him aware of His presence in Moses' life. He sent Moses on a mission to bring the Israelites out of Egypt. Moses would have to stand before the most powerful man in the world with all his fear, doubt, insecurity, and uncertainty and demand God's people be set free. This is definitely nowhere in Moses' plan.

Matter of fact, Moses argues with God about it. It was so against the plan, that Moses argued and made excuses. "Who am I to stand against Pharaoh? Why is anyone going to listen to me? What if they don't believe that you came to me? You know I can't speak well." Translation, "This is not the plan. Not what I had in mind. Is there another option? Maybe someone else?"

God prepared him and God positioned him. And where he lacked faith, God empowered him and equipped him. And through him, God would do immeasurably more than Moses could ever think or even imagine. That is the ultimate story. Our God is the one who can do immeasurably more through our lives. He is the God of creation. The God of Abraham, Isaac, and Jacob. The God of Moses. The God of Israel. And He is the same yesterday, today, and forever.

He is preparing you, positioning you. He is equipping you and He will empower you. He desires to work through you in just the same way. The story of Moses isn't just a dusty old Bible story, made up sometime, somewhere. It isn't just for "back then." It is the story of God. It is written for us to understand Him. It is written for us to relate, and you can find yourself in that story.

Fast forward from Moses to Summer 2012. We came home from that interview and sat in the living room. Silent. Confused. More questions than answers. Where do we go now? What do we do next? It wouldn't be long before everything would change. We just had no idea how. This wasn't the plan.

Jennifer spent some time checking job postings again. There was another science job opening at Sparkman Middle. I had not really wanted that for Jennifer. We both thought Discovery was a better fit for her. I heard, in my time at Sparkman 9, that Sparkman Middle was a challenging place to teach. I had mentioned the job to Jennifer just a few days prior. I was only gauging her interest in the possibility of applying. She didn't seem to have very much. Of course, when you set your mind on what you see as a better option, it is hard to settle for something lesser. Contentment is a hard lesson for Americans.

Moses was probably just fine in his own world in Midian...the problems of Israelite slaves in Egypt long forgotten. That is, until God called him back. Even still, the option of Egypt presented to Moses wasn't such a glorious plan in his own eyes. God has a way of calling us to do things that just don't seem like the best option in our own minds.

We sat there that afternoon in our living room...dejected, confused, uncertain. And honestly, there was doubt, a lot of doubt, in my head anyways. What is the deal? Why would this not work out for her? For us? Do we not deserve something better? Why couldn't God just let her have this job? Does He not care about our future? Our happiness?

I had been searching the job market for Jennifer every day. I knew every job that was out there that she was qualified for, when it opened, and when it closed. And the only one left was that job at Sparkman Middle. I remember sitting on the couch, Jennifer standing in the doorway to our living room, when I was compelled to ask her this question, I believe by the Holy Spirit. In the middle of all those feelings of rejection, "Do you want to apply for that job at Sparkman Middle or not? It closes today." And the end of today was getting close. In fact, we were already well into the afternoon.

There we were, sitting in front of our only, not so glorious option. It's not according to the plan. It wasn't even on the board of possibilities. But it's the only door left open. And there is a good chance we are walking toward a door that isn't even open. I have been around education long enough to know that by the time that job posting closes, that job is typically already spoken for.

The not so sure reply came from across the room as Jennifer said, "Well, I guess so." She sat down and sent an email to Ronnie Blair, at the time, principal at Sparkman Middle. Within ten minutes she had applied for the job. Within thirty minutes she had received a phone call. Within an hour, she was at the school interviewing with Mr. Blair and Mrs. Teresa Terrell, assistant principal.

I am not even sure it was an interview as much as Mrs. Terrell "sold" Jennifer on the job. She made her feel so welcome. Mrs. Terrell had a gift for that. She was like "Mom" to everyone.

I was home when Jennifer called. She had been in there about 45 minutes. It is rare that you go to a school for an interview, see the room you will teach in, and walk out of the interview with a textbook in hand. It didn't take them long to figure out she was special. She has that effect on people.

Jennifer became the newest teacher at Sparkman Middle School in Toney, Alabama that day. We had no idea why. No idea where it was going, or what it would become. We had no idea how great a challenge it would be. We had no idea what we were getting into. It was never any part of the plan...even when it was all that was left.

That decision would end up being a huge one for us. We didn't even recognize God's hand in moving

Jennifer there at the time; but it would prove to be a decision that would change our lives. It would change our perspective on life. It would change our view of God. It would change the way we saw the world. And we weren't looking for any of that. We were just looking for an extra income.

God was positioning us, just like He did Moses thousands of years before. He was preparing us. He was going to equip us and empower us. Through Jennifer accepting that job, He was going to show that He is the God of immeasurably more than all we can ask, think, or even imagine, just like He was to Moses. And just like the story of Moses, our plan wasn't the plan that mattered. God's plan wasn't even an option for us. How is that for immeasurably more? His perfect plan wasn't even on our list of options. We never dreamed about His plan. It never even made a blip on our radar screen. Interestingly enough, I think Moses would tell you the same thing about God's work in his life. He is the God of more. Maybe we should learn to seek His plan.

2

Lord, What Do You Want Me To Do?

All I ever really wanted to do was be a basketball coach. I was the kid who played ball twenty-four seven. I rode my bike to the rec center or got my parents to drop me off and leave me there all day during the summer. It was my life. I remember going to the high school gym in the mornings to shoot by myself. We had a huge gym and I would be out there shooting over a ten-foot ladder. Two hundred threes. Three hundred. Sometimes five hundred. Every now and then, one of the custodians, Jimmy Speegle, would come in and rebound for me. He really just liked to talk, but I didn't mind. I have worked in quite a few schools now...some things are true everywhere you go.

After I got my shots up, I would jog over to the rec center, which was not even a mile from my school, to find a pickup game. In Tullahoma, Tennessee if you were a kid that played basketball, the only places to find a pickup game on a summer day were D.W. Wilson and C.D. Stamps Community Centers. And the time was shortly after lunch. All the other high school kids were at summer football workouts and baseball games, so I was finding pickup games with older guys in the community. Looking back, it was probably a pretty clear sign to my parents that those guys were playing ball at the rec center at 1:00 when they should have been working. That might clue you in on how they were paying the bills. But I didn't care. They could play and they were playing...and that was all I cared about.

The Lord was really watching over me at the time. I had no idea what I was getting into. Several of those guys have been in and out of jail. A couple of them taken at a really young age. You can imagine the circumstances. Needless to say, He protected me. In large part due to some of those guys. Much credit to Joe Moon, who ran D.W. Wilson for a long, long time. Joe was a good guy. He really had a heart for people and especially all those guys. He kept them in line, challenged them to be better, and used his influence in that place for good. Joe passed from this life in 2016. He was hit by a car running at an extremely high rate of speed. It was being pursued by police. A young person was driving that car, twenty-one. Ironic...Joe had spent his life pouring into young people like that. Just another tragedy as a result of the broken world we live in. Thank God for people like Joe who are committed to making an impact for good.

Looking back, I think my love for the game of basketball came from the Lord. I certainly could have been much better at something else. There aren't a whole lot of white guys under six feet advancing their careers as basketball players. Interestingly enough, I am the only male under six feet on both sides of my family. My brother, Ben, was taller than me when he was twelve. I was nineteen. My dad towers over me and he has a brother that towers over him. Point in case, basketball wasn't the game for me to fall in love with, but it's still one of my passions.

I learned life through the game of basketball. I was really fortunate. And no part of it was easy, but looking back on it I wouldn't trade it for anything. I would rather know what I know today by walking through what I had to walk through, than have had it any other way.

Basketball taught me what so many people learn through sports, music, etc. Things like the value of hard work, self-discipline, and being able to work with others. I am grateful for each of those lessons, but the positions the Lord put me in through the game of basketball taught me so much more.

I played for four coaches in high school. I didn't enjoy playing for any of them. I didn't have much respect for any of them. Coaches often have egos. I speak from experience. Coaches often are motivated by accomplishments, winning, trophies and banners. I speak from experience. We all want to win. We all live in our own world. We all think what we are doing is the biggest thing on the face of the earth in the moment. And sometimes, all those things come out in the way we treat people. I can totally relate. I've made all those mistakes and more.

But the greatest thing I learned from four high school basketball coaches in four years was that I didn't want to be like any of them. I didn't want to be a person that prioritized his world over everyone else's around him. I didn't want to respond to people out of anger, frustration, with the intent to humiliate, ridicule, or embarrass. I didn't want to be insensitive to the emotions of other people. I didn't want people's impression of me to be "my way or the highway." And I didn't want to use my words to destroy people, be it through sarcasm, bullying, cursing, belittling, or whatever else. Life is too short to be on my own journey. It's too short to spend it prioritizing success at the expense of other people. It's too short for me to spend it thinking I have all the answers.

There may not have ever been a truer statement about dealing with people than, "nobody cares how much you know, until they know how much you care." I got to learn how true that statement was firsthand. The Lord gave me coaches that weren't very interested in being role models. They were interested in being dictators. I learned much in those four years without even realizing what I was learning. I was learning about life. It was hard. And I wanted to quit. Through it all the Lord gave me a relentless spirit and awareness. The ability to be aware of how my words and actions impact other people. I am grateful for that. Extremely grateful for that.

My senior year was the most difficult of all. We had an extremely talented team my junior year. That team won a lot of basketball games. I was the only starter on that team that wasn't a senior. They all graduated and two of our juniors were not on the team our senior year. Jamil Northcutt signed a football scholarship to Ole Miss and chose not to play. He was a natural leader. Brad

Chedister's dad took a job at the Pentagon and his family moved. Brad was probably our best player coming back. We had two seniors on the team and I was the only player with significant experience returning. Our new coach elected to play for the future and brought up freshman and sophomores to rely on. I still played quite a bit, but it wasn't the same for sure. We won six games that year. Brutal.

We were playing our rivals one night at home. We were down ten or so with just a couple of minutes left. Our coach was notorious for humiliating us in front of the crowd. I guess he had to make sure everyone knew it wasn't his fault. This was one of those moments. He called a timeout and said, "Y'all won't listen to me, so figure it out yourselves." Then he went and sat on the end of the bench for the remainder of the game.

It was one of those God moments...maybe to send him a message. I don't know. But we won that game. I remember it like it was yesterday. He walked out of the huddle and the first thing out of my mouth was, "He hasn't ever cared about us anyway. Who cares about him." Of course, he decided to coach again as we started to rally. But another thing I have learned is that some people are only capable of looking out for themselves. I don't have to judge it, I just need to be aware of it.

That moment is a microcosm of my high school basketball career. In fact, when it is was over...I was over it. It was the game that I loved and I just wanted away from it.

Another thing the Lord gave me through basketball was understanding. Basketball is a game that thrives anywhere because it can played anywhere by anybody. You can find a basketball and a hoop just about anywhere, and that is all you need. It doesn't take a whole lot of money to create a pickup game.

Because of all those reasons, basketball allowed me opportunities to see a whole lot of things up close that I may have never paid attention to otherwise. My family wasn't wealthy, but we weren't poor either. We were a middle-class American family. My sister and I didn't get cars when we turned sixteen like many of our friends. My parents didn't buy us all the brand name clothes and shoes and whatever else. They struggled to pay the bills sometimes, but they always found a way and we had what we needed.

The guys I played ball with...not always. It's one thing to share a locker room with those guys and be on a team with those guys. It's another thing to value them, embrace them, and live life with them. The Lord gave me a gift to have a heart for people...their situations...their needs. I valued them. I embraced them. And I lived life with them.

Perspective changes when you are the guy that takes your teammate home and realize his deal isn't at all like yours. When you are the guy that is dropping him off at 11:30 at night to an empty house because his mom is out running the streets and his dad lives less than five miles away and has nothing to do with him, that's a pretty tough reality. Or when you realize that he is having you drop him in the wrong part of town because he feels a burden to provide money for his single mom who is trying to raise three kids and he only knows one way to do that. I saw some painful situations and I clearly remember the impact those situations had on me when I was young.

Jesus looked out over the multitude and had compassion because they were like "sheep without a shepherd." If I had a nickel for every sheep without a shepherd that I have met through the game of basketball. Breaks my heart. Broke my heart when I was in high school. Breaks my heart still today. A whole lot of sheep out there without a shepherd, and for some reason, even at the age of sixteen, I have always felt a burden to be the shepherd. Maybe that is from the Lord too.

In fact, I am sitting here writing this story, in my new job at Madison Academy. I came here to teach Bible. I came here because I felt the Lord was calling me to this place and to this role of teaching others about Him. I love my job. I talk about Jesus every day, all day. And I still feel a burden to be somewhere else with the sheep that have no shepherd.

A couple of years away from basketball and my passion was renewed. I had originally gone to school to pursue a computer science degree. My sophomore year of college was when my heart led me to coaching basketball. It would also lead me to UAH to work for Lennie Acuff. Coach Acuff was the polar opposite of all my high school coaches.

He is a phenomenal coach, but an even better person. Other basketball coaches still ask me what the greatest thing I learned from Coach Acuff was. My answer has always been the same, "to value and appreciate everyone." It's fun to watch their response. I think they expect an answer about backdoor cuts or the Princeton offense. Coach Acuff is successful because of the way he treats people. He could run any offense, anytime, anywhere and be successful. He just knows how to lead people because he values people.

To this day, when I am teaching class and the custodian comes in to take out the trash, I always stop teaching, call them by name, and say, "Thank you for that." And every time, I think about Coach Acuff. I am grateful for his influence, whether I ever coach another basketball game or not.

Basketball was my dream again. My goal was to be a high school basketball coach. Everything I did was toward that career goal. In fact, when I went to teach at Sparkman 9, it was so I could coach at Sparkman High School. I thought if I was an assistant coach at one of the biggest high schools in the state, it would open doors for me to get where I was going, and I was ready to get there. Sparkman High was going to get me there.

I stayed at Sparkman High as an assistant for two years. Two challenging years. Being a high school coach is tough. It's like having two full time jobs, at least, if you value being a good classroom teacher also. Coaching at Sparkman High taught me one thing...I wasn't exactly cut out for it. It's hard to walk away from my family during

Holidays for basketball games. It's hard to leave them at home during winter break to play Thanksgiving tournaments and Christmas tournaments. It's hard to be sitting on a bench at 8:00 in the evening in Decatur, knowing they are going to bed without me home. Maybe it's that whole "sheep without a shepherd" thing.

Either way, the Lord just took that desire away from my heart. I had spent all my life wanting to be a basketball coach and now I didn't really care anymore. In fact, I wasn't sure what I wanted. Where was I going? What was I doing? What were my career goals? I felt like I had lost my identity. Now what?

The Bible tells a similar story in Acts 9. It's about a man named Saul. Saul knew what he wanted to do with his life also. His family had been very attached to the Pharisaic traditions. Paul was sent to Jerusalem where he would be educated at the feet of Gamaliel, a great rabbi. Paul was educated, far beyond what most people were in his day.

He is introduced in the Bible as a persecutor of the church. He was making a name for himself in doing so. He was establishing a reputation. He was traveling all over making sure those "Christians" suffered. Beatings, imprisonments, death, it didn't matter as long as they were put in their place. Saul knew what he was doing, where he was going, and how he was going to get there. Well, that is, until the Lord met him on the way to Damascus. As he was on his way, carrying letters from the high priest to the synagogues of Damascus giving him the authority to bring followers of Jesus back to Jerusalem, Saul was met by Jesus.

It was Jesus who would ask him, "Why do you persecute Me?" (Acts 9:4 NIV). Saul recognized Him as Lord, immediately. "Who are you, Lord?" (Acts 9:5 NIV). And the only other question he had for Him, "Lord, what do you want me to do?"

It was then that Saul would become Paul the apostle. He would spend the remainder of his time on earth on mission for the Lord. Travelling all over, carrying the gospel to the Gentile world, planting churches, and leading the movement of Christianity. He is the most important person in the Apostolic Age. He wrote half the letters of the New Testament. All because he asked the question, "Lord, what do you want me to do?"

Jennifer had a great first year at Sparkman Middle. While she was there, I was still working at Sparkman 9. This was my third year at Sparkman 9. It was my first year out of coaching. I had missed it some, but for the most part, I was enjoying the year off.

At year's end, Sparkman Middle was looking for a boys' basketball coach. Jennifer had actually grown fond of several of the boys on that team through having them in class. She really wanted me to come over to the middle school to coach.

The reputation at the high school was that Sparkman Middle kids were great athletes but, in general, weren't coachable, didn't know how to be team players, and didn't work hard. Some of that was stereotype and some of it was just a product of nobody investing in them. Either way, it was calling to me. They were like sheep without a shepherd.

I joined Jennifer at the middle school, the place that neither of us wanted to be. The same place that was a last resort would end up becoming a home for us. Strange how things work out sometimes. Those years were three of our happiest years. We were working beside each other, investing in those sheep, and building a culture there together. We were a family. The kids of SMS were like our children. In fact, that whole faculty was like a family, raising many of those kids. So many of those people were a huge blessing in our lives.

It was easy to see why the Lord called me there for those three years. I was able to coach several talented kids. We had some good teams. We lost in the finals of the County Tournament every year I was there. But that wasn't why the Lord called me there.

I coached so many kids there that were fatherless. I coached so many kids there that had no male figure in their life. That was my calling. I approached every day like I was raising those boys. Teaching them responsibility, work ethic, team. Teaching them about Jesus and what He calls us to be and how He calls us to love, praying with them, taking them to serve in their community. Trying to be an example to them of what life is all about.

The Lord called me back to basketball, but for His glory. So many people asked me why in the world I went to SMS. It was a tough, challenging job. It didn't really make sense compared to the job I had. But I loved it. I loved working with my wife. I loved the fact that those middle school kids embraced our son, Ty. I loved being in a lower stress environment. Coaching was fun again, because the Lord had taken my heart for basketball and given me a heart for those kids.

My strength didn't come from myself. It didn't come from basketball, or from winning. My strength came from the Lord (Psalm 121:3 NIV), and what He called me to do and where He called me to be, at least in that moment.

Paul had a desire to serve the Lord his whole life. It was just misguided before he came to know Jesus. The Lord gave him the qualities he needed. He prepared the way before him. He gave him the ability to relate to Jew and Gentile. He gave him the education he would need, the passion, the work ethic. He even gave Paul some of these things by allowing him to go the wrong direction. But God protected Paul, and when the time was right, He moved to bring Paul where He desired for him to be and equipped him to do what He was called to do. All in response to Paul's question, "Lord, what do you want me to do?"

The God of the Bible, the God that called Paul, is the same God that called me. Paul's story is my story. I've learned from my story that God let me go down the path I desired. He used that path to prepare me for the moment when I would say, 'Lord, what do You want me to do?' He is the same yesterday, today, and forever. He is writing my story just as He did Paul's. He has gone before me.

Paul didn't know what would happen after that question was answered, but he knew the answer to that question was greater than anything he could plan or purpose for himself. And that was exactly why he asked the question. What do I learn from this? I don't want to do anything in my life that isn't directly related to the answer to that question. That's why I keep asking, "Lord, What do you want me to do?"

3

Learning He Provides

The years that Jennifer and I worked together at SMS were some of the best times. Even now, when I drive down Jeff Road and pull up toward the school, it brings up some of the best memories. The coworkers we had at SMS were some of the best people we knew. It was a tremendous family and we were blessed to be a part of it.

Jennifer has a way with people. She has a gift for making everyone feel appreciated and valued. God gave her a "shepherd" gifting. She has a knack for understanding how people are feeling and how to be a blessing to them. God gave her opportunities to use that gift at SMS to bring people together. It really is an incredible thing to witness.

The greatest thing that Jennifer did at Sparkman Middle School was to start a school food pantry. The Lord put that need on her heart and there were so many children there that were blessed by that. There were Fridays that the food bag providers didn't show up and Jennifer's little classroom pantry would provide for over fifty kids. There were times when there weren't enough food bags for all the kids that needed them and that little pantry in her closet would have just enough for some children who we had just found out about.

That food pantry was the beginning of us understanding just how much need was in our community. Still, to this day, when I tell people about the situation in the Harvest/Toney area they say, "I had no idea how much need was out there." Truth is, at the time, we had no idea either. But the Lord was showing us more and more about how much need there really was and at the same time, He was giving us more and more understanding as to why He brought us there.

That food pantry evolving really changed everything about us. We began to see the world in a different light...all of us did. It really impacted our entire family. It is amazing how your entire deal can change with just a little shift in perspective.

I remember how the Lord brought so many needs to our attention just through that little food pantry and how He made it so easy for us to be able to provide for those needs...effortlessly at times. We went from providing peanut butter crackers to helping children get clothing, coats, glasses, and even beds. It really was remarkable how the Lord would put it on someone's heart to provide every need we met.

The children would break your heart. Seeing the things that they were willing to do even for each other was incredible. There was one time that Jennifer gave a boy a coat and he asked her if he could trade it for another one. Her first thought was that he was being picky, but she let him choose anyway. He swapped that coat for another coat that had a liner in it that you could unzip and take out. After he made the exchange, he unzipped the coat put on the liner, and gave the coat part to his little brother. How is that for understanding the heart of God at a young age? Reminds me of these verses, "Do nothing out of selfish ambition or vain conceit. Rather, in humility value others above yourselves, not looking to your own interests but each of you to the interests of others" (Philippians 2:3-

4 NIV). It's funny how children can see the world so simply. No wonder Jesus said we should "receive the kingdom like a little child" (Mark 10:15 NIV).

It was in Exodus 16 that the people of Israel began to gripe and fuss at Moses and Aaron in the wilderness. They had been caught wandering there for some time after they had been led out of captivity in Egypt. The people began to complain and some even desired to be back in Egypt. They even began proclaiming that Moses had brought them out of Egypt to die of hunger in the wilderness.

The Bible tells us that the Lord heard their complaints and was prepared to show them, yet again as He had in Egypt and at the Red Sea, that He was their God. It was God's desire that they would know. You would think, by this point, they would have learned how to trust in and rely on God, but that doesn't seem to be the case. It's funny how we need to be taught the same lesson multiple times. It's so hard for us to focus on God in the middle of life, even when we have seen the miraculous. It actually gives me comfort that the Israelites struggled with that too.

As it was, the Lord provided for them daily. Bread in the form of manna from heaven each morning and quail meat in the evening is what the Lord would provide for His children. Every single day, the people of Israel were able to witness how God was providing for them. It's an incredible statement to God's power and desire to provide...even when the Israelites were at their worst.

Truth is, we were witnessing the same things daily. We watched as God just put it on people's hearts to meet need after need. Sometimes it was food, sometimes it was glasses, coats, and even beds that we were able to get to children in need just by them bringing up their need. It was a remarkable time for us, and our faith was growing daily. I remember thinking at times that it was like we were speaking things into existence. God was so faithful to provide.

I remember one day taking a phone call during my planning period. I was out walking around the school just spending some time by myself when my phone rang. The person on the line was telling me how they needed a window air conditioning unit. Their house was intensely hot, but they were unable to afford getting the air fixed. I had no idea what to tell them. We had a few appliances that had been donated in the past but that wasn't really what we did or wanted to do. In fact, we wouldn't take them unless we had somewhere for them to go immediately. We just didn't have a way to store things.

I hung up the phone thinking, "What in the world. Why would someone think I could help them find an air conditioner? That makes zero sense." I walked inside and sat down at my desk to check my email. In my inbox there was an email sent while I was walking. It was a lady who wanted to donate a window unit air conditioner. It has been over four years since we started the food pantry at SMS and, to this day, we have had one air conditioner donated and one request for an air conditioner...within about five minutes of each other.

Our lives began to have so many situations like this that it was impossible to not realize what God was doing. I would literally be in conversation with someone and tell them something we needed for the food pantry and then my phone would ring and the person on the other end would have that item to donate...with no idea that we were even in need of it. There was no denying...God was at work and He was providing in overwhelming ways. It really was incredible.

It was through all these experiences that I learned that the God of the Bible, is the God of today. He loves the same, provides the same, and answers prayers the same. He knows our needs before we do and He desires for us to know how much He cares. The God who provided the manna for the Israelites, that I can read about in Exodus 16, is the God who supplied that pantry at Sparkman Middle School in 2015. He dropped every can of peanut butter, every granola bar, and every pop-tart, every coat, pair of glasses, bed, washing machine, and every air conditioner, just like He did in the wilderness.

4

The God Who Multiplies

That little food pantry Jennifer started in her class room would end up being the beginning of great things. What is funny is that none of us intended for it to grow. We didn't have a three-year plan or a five-year plan for it to become more than it was. We didn't cast a short-term and long-term vision. We really didn't even have an awareness that there was more that was needed than we were able to provide. She saw an immediate need and she was willing to seek to meet it to the best of her ability, all out of love for the students of Sparkman Middle School.

It was only after the pantry had been depleted and restocked multiple times over that we started to see that we couldn't really keep up. But God had been working behind the scenes all along, throughout this whole process in ways that we couldn't see or understand. One of the first things we did when that little cabinet was empty was call on our church at the Light to restock it. I still remember going to church that following Sunday to see Brad Minor's truck full of food that would more than fill that cabinet. He and his wife, Angie, had collected donations from everyone and had gone to purchase all of that food. They stocked that cabinet three times over.

Jennifer and I drove those donations out to SMS that Sunday afternoon in awe. We were so amazed at how people responded to the need for children and families that they didn't even know. But, sure enough, there we were making trip after trip from the truck to Jennifer's classroom with loads of food. I look back and laugh now because we couldn't believe it. That was such a small blessing compared to the things that we have been able to see God do today, but at that time we thought it was the most unbelievable thing. I distinctly remember that situation bringing me so much joy that we were at the Light and God was beginning to teach me that He can meet any need.

It was a special time for me. I had actually been preaching part time at a church in Huntsville that I had been attending since I was in college. I had a great deal invested there and leaving was hard for multiple reasons, but it was the right thing. My beliefs weren't lining up with the leadership there and I just didn't need to be a part. I was becoming more of a distraction to the direction they were going. It was hard to give up the extra income. It was hard to leave all I had known since being in Huntsville. And it was hard to give up the position as well. I realize I shouldn't feel that way, but that is just total transparency. But God works in all of it. Through that experience He taught me not to value position or status. It's not about me anyway. Every opportunity I have to lead, teach, or speak is an opportunity to send His message forward and glorify His name. I was too spiritually immature to embrace that at the time.

When we left that church, I was really lost. I was learning that I didn't understand relationship with God at all. I may have understood some context of religion, but I had a lot to learn about God, His message, His Kingdom and what it meant for my life. I was really lost. In fact, I was so lost that all I knew to do was go to church with the best ambassadors for the kingdom of God that I knew. To me, those people were at a little church called the Light. As it turns out, the Light was a little lost too. In fact, a good friend of ours, Andy Blackston, put it like this, "You guys chose the Light at a time when that wasn't a popular choice." He was right. God used the Light to help us rewire our thinking and God used us to re-energize the Light. Looking back, it was a huge blessing to be a part of. It was a time that God stamped His message on my heart.

He is so faithful. Looking back, one of the biggest struggles I had was giving up what seemed to be so much at the time. Four years later, God has restored it all. He has given us better relationships, an opportunity to do real ministry in the real lives of real people every Saturday morning, opportunities for me to speak at the Light on occasion, and so many different arenas where He has called Jennifer and me to lead others. It was Job who said, "The Lord gave and the Lord has taken away. Blessed be the name of the Lord" (Job 1:21 NIV).

Let me get back to the SMS food pantry. It wasn't long before God would surprise us again. In the background, while all this is going on, the Lord had really put it on my heart to go and spend time volunteering at the Manna House in Huntsville. In fact, the Lord had put it on my heart through the words of another person. I was at the Light one Sunday morning listening to another good friend, Brian Privett, preach when he said, "If Jesus were here today, places like the Manna House are where He would be spending His time." I had no idea what the Manna House was, but that statement was enough to make me want to find out about it. In fact, to this day, I am not really sure why Brian made that statement. I don't remember where it fit in his message. I don't remember what his message was about, but that one sentence caught my heart because of where I was. I was seeking God more than at any other point in my life in that moment.

I look back at this moment as life-changing for me. I could have probably heard those same words another day and time and just looked right past them. The Holy Spirit used those words this particular day and the next day I was at the Manna House, seeking to find God, be where He would be, and be involved in what He was doing. This is one of the very qualities about Jesus that I admire most. Jesus spent His time on earth watching what God the Father was doing. He chose to use His time joining the Father where He was working. I want to imitate this more than anything. It was about this time in my life when I really started to realize how much "at work" God really is. The fact of the matter is, He had always been working, I just hadn't been aware of it. I was so used to the God I was taught growing up, the One that wasn't active today. Now, I pray daily for eyes to see where God is working. I don't want to miss any opportunities to experience Him in my daily life.

It didn't take long for God to start making connections. The first time I walked in the door at the Manna House, I saw Thor Erlingson. Thor had been my roommate for a year in college when he had first come over to the United States from Iceland. He has a remarkable story and God has used him in incredible ways. We had not really talked in several years. We had seen each other around some, but hadn't really had a chance to spend time together. Thor really welcomed me at the Manna House and I began to spend at least one day a week there over the course of the next several months. In fact, it became a special place to me in that season of my life. I would invite friends to go with me and we would volunteer together and get to spend some time catching up. I would be able to spend time with Thor and hear the stories of what God was doing in his life. I'll never forget taking our son, Ty, to the Manna House to volunteer with me. He was probably about 5 at the time. He was still struggling with talking. Ty began talking really late. In fact, his speech therapist encouraged us to invest in an $8,000 communication device because of the strong possibility he would never speak. God had different plans for him, though. Back to the Manna House and one of my fondest memories, as Ty was sitting on my shoulders handing out jelly to the people on the other side of the line. He didn't quite have his l-sound together yet, as he asked every person, "You want some jerry?"

Through all of these moments, I was also getting to know people whose influence was changing my life. Fran Fluhler, the director at the Manna House, has impacted my life as much as anyone I have ever known. Spending time around her at a crucial time for me really was a huge part of shaping my faith in the God who does immeasurably more than we can ask, dream, or imagine. God introduced me to lifelong friends like Jeff and Lisa Burgess in my time at the Manna House. I look back and see how much God was teaching me. He was showing me things about the way He loves us. He was helping me to understand the way He thinks and His heart for the brokenness of people. He was teaching me how to be present and to minister to people and how to trust in Him to provide the material things that were needed. I have probably been one of His slowest learners, but I am grateful that He never gave up on me.

There was so much life that I was experiencing in those weekly trips to the Manna House that it really became one of the highlights of my week. I started taking my basketball teams over to work and seeing the energy from the kids when they were able to be involved. It really did change so much about the way I think and the understanding God was giving me for what life and serving Him is all about. Brian was right when he spoke those words in that sermon and I am grateful that the Lord put those words before me.

It was a casual conversation with Thor that ignited the growth of our little classroom food cabinet. It was depleted again and I was telling Thor about it when he said, "Can I come out there tomorrow?" I replied, "Sure," with no idea what was on his mind. The next day Jennifer, Shalunda Sherrod (the school's behavior specialist), Thor, Donald Walker, and I sat down in the Sparkman Middle Library where we would discuss how to provide what our students at SMS needed.

I don't remember much about that meeting today other than Thor saying, very clearly, "Don't worry about the food. The food will be here. There is plenty of food. You need to be more concerned about where to put the food." And he spoke that with so much faith that we all began to get the feeling that something was about to happen. Even at this point, speaking for myself, my faith was not at a place that recognized that God was doing something and that He really had His hand in what was happening. I was learning about God and only beginning to experience Him.

We walked away from that meeting and God just started making things easy. It's a good thing too, because I had no idea what I was doing and if He hadn't made it so easy, I would have probably messed everything up. Looking back on it, I am amazed that I didn't.

In the next few weeks, our principal at the time, Ronnie Blair, would offer us an empty classroom to use to store the food we had because the cabinet (that we couldn't keep full) was not big enough to hold all the food we had. In just a few short days, we had a classroom that was full of shelves stocked up with food. It was like a grocery store inside the school.

That little move multiplied what we were able to do and the number of students we were able to serve. It also multiplied how many hands were able to be involved with what we were doing. Like clockwork, every week, Thor would drive a load of food out to SMS and my basketball players would unload it into that classroom. Jennifer and her SGA club would come along and organize it onto the shelves. On Wednesday night a regular group of volunteers from the Light would drive out to SMS, pack boxes, and take them to the homes of students where we would sit down with their families and make connections and build relationships.

There were times that it was hard. There were times that we couldn't do all the work. But we kept being faithful to that, week in and week out, for several months. I even remember taking days off work because we had boxes that didn't get delivered. But, I look back at that time and think God was testing our faithfulness because what He was about to do next was big and He had to make sure He could trust us with it.

It was in Genesis 22 that God asked Abraham to sacrifice his only son, Isaac. Actually Isaac was the son that God had promised Abraham a long time before. Isaac was the son that God promised Abraham He would bless the nations of the earth through. Abraham had waited for 25 years from the time that God made that promise just for Isaac to be born. Can you imagine God telling you that He was going to do something in your life and then twenty-five years later, He still hasn't done it yet? Father, increase my faith. Can you imagine God telling you that through your offspring, all nations would be blessed and you are 99 years old and without a child? Then, the child is finally born, years go by, and now God wants Abraham to literally sacrifice him there as a burnt offering?

I can't imagine all the things that went through Abraham's mind the night before and on into that morning. But there were two things going on. Scripture says that God tested Abraham. He wanted to see if He was willing. The conclusion for God, "Now I know that you fear God because you have not withheld from Me your son, your only son" (Genesis 22:12 NIV). That was the first thing, God was testing Abraham. But also, over in Hebrews 11, it tells us what was going on in Abraham's mind. Scripture tells us that Abraham, "reasoned that God could even raise the dead" (Hebrews 11:19 NIV).

Abraham didn't know what God was doing. He didn't understand why. But he did know that God could do whatever He wanted and Abraham put his trust in that, even when it didn't make sense. As a result, God knew that He could trust Abraham. Abraham was willing to obey, even when He didn't understand. He was willing to carry out what he had been called to, even when it didn't make sense. He was trusting God through his test. They were learning to trust each other.

When I look back on our story, I see God testing us by asking for a sacrifice. There were some days when we didn't understand why we were doing what we were doing. There were days that it didn't make a whole lot of sense to be driving back and forth to the Manna House to pick up loads of food, or tracking down boxes so that we would have something to pack the food in, and taking days off of work to make sure we got food delivered to every house that we had committed to. There were times when the sacrifice of my time, energy, and resources made me question why in the world we were doing it. But I knew in my mind, I was going to honor every commitment. In Jennifer's mind, we were going to meet every need that was brought to our attention.

At the time, I don't think we would have articulated that God had called us to it, but I do think that we felt a supernatural urge from the Holy Spirit to see every need through. I distinctly remember thinking at times that those kids weren't going to be hungry because I didn't hold up my end of the deal. Most of those kids had plenty of adults in their life who weren't holding up their end of the deal and I was determined not to be added to that list.

Looking back, I absolutely think that God was testing us. He was trying to see how committed we were. Are you going to unload that truck when you have do it by yourself? Are you going to go pick up that food when it can't be delivered at the last minute and you are the only answer? Are you going to make sure that food gets on that table where you said it was...every time? Or are you going to get distracted by what you want to do today? Tomorrow? Next week? When someone else drops the ball on their part are you going to blame them or get the job done?

It was a test. A test to see if we were prepared for what He had planned for that little cabinet. He is the God of immeasurably more. He was preparing to show that to us, but He had to make sure we were the right ones first. He had to see if we were willing to trust Him with our last Two Fish.

It seems trivial to compare sacrificing your only son to the sacrifice of time, energy, and resources that God was testing us with. It also seems trivial to run a food pantry compared to being the father of the nation through which all nations of the earth would be blessed. God had a huge task for Abraham and He gave Abraham a huge test. Here is the thing, He is the same God that He was yesterday. He gave Abraham a test and He gave Abraham responsibility. I believe with all of my heart that God did the same thing with Jennifer and me and all those who are committed to our mission with us. He gave us a test. Had we failed the test, I wouldn't be writing this book. That classroom food cabinet would have remained just what it was. But instead, He blessed our effort. He is the God of immeasurably more. He is the God who can multiply two fish into twelve baskets of leftovers...and that hasn't changed, and it won't change.

5

Pre-Determined

We packed those boxes in that classroom once a week for what seemed like several months. We delivered food to those families every Wednesday night faithfully. I don't know that we even knew what we were doing when we first started. We had chosen twelve families from Sparkman Middle School that were in need of some assistance and were willing to allow us to come to their homes.

Every one of those situations was pretty desperate. I remember grandparents who were struggling to raise their grandchildren because the parents weren't, a single father of a teenage daughter who couldn't work because cancer was destroying his body and all he had ever learned was how to work with his hands, single moms who had been left behind with three children in school and could only work during school hours. There were all kinds of situations that would just break your heart, each one unique and each one completely tragic. What is really interesting is that all the families we were helping were doing their best. Getting involved with those families was an experience that really opened my eyes to different people's situations.

As the weeks went by, we started to get phone calls from the other schools in the Sparkman High zone about the families they had in need. Pretty soon we were up to thirty families that we were delivering boxes to on a weekly basis. We were literally mapping out where all these families lived to try and find the best routes for people to deliver two and three boxes on Wednesday nights. All of us were taken aback by how much need there was.

While all of this was going on, I was communicating with Thor about how much food we needed and how that need is constantly increasing. Finally one day, Thor sent Jennifer and me to the Manna House to talk to Fran. We went that afternoon. Our dilemma was that the number of families needing our services was growing by the day but we couldn't continue to do what we were doing because we were pushing our deliverers to the limit already. As long as we were delivering, the number of people delivering would have to grow with the number of boxes going out.

Fran has been doing this for a long time. In fact, at this point, the Manna House had been operating in its' current building for almost ten years, and she had been feeding God's children in Madison County, Alabama for more like thirty. Never mind the fact that Fran was already established in her faith in the God that can do immeasurably more.

As we stood there with her that afternoon, in a very matter of fact way, she simply stated, 'You need a building." Sure thing, right? Just like that. Go find a building. No sweat. Two teachers with a family. Just go find a building. No worries. Problem solved.

Jennifer and I walked out with no idea how that would happen, yet with belief that it was supposed to happen. This was one of those moments that Jesus talks about, you know, "According to your faith, let it be done to you" (Matthew 9:29 NIV). Fran had no doubt. I wish I could say Jennifer and I were anywhere near as confident. Needless to say, I think God put us in that moment for us to learn faith like Fran's. In fact, "faith like Fran" would become a common phrase in our house. I guess at the time, our faith was not even the size of a mustard seed.

I went home that night and looked at buildings for rent in the Harvest area. I was already trying to find a solution that made more sense. Maybe we could afford to rent one for a few short months and determine if this is actually going to work or not. That sounds like a much more realistic, logical, and practical plan. Little did I know, God doesn't work in my reality, logic, or practicality. He was yet to teach me that my ways don't compare to His. The Bible clearly makes this statement (Isaiah 55:8-9), but I am really bad about having to experience things for myself.

I couldn't find much for rent, but I accidentally stumbled upon one for sale that was perfect. It belonged to the Harvest Fire Department. It was in a perfect location in Harvest, that everyone had known for years and that everyone passed frequently. It was a warehouse style building with garage doors, lots of floor space. It was exactly what we needed, where we needed it to be, and available....for $220,000. And that was the problem.

Paying for that building really wasn't an option for us. But maybe, for what we were doing, they would let us rent it? Or just use it for a few months? The worst they can do is tell us, "No," right? Fortunately for us, the secretary for the Fire Department was also a bus driver for the school. Cathy Vanbentheuysen was someone I had gotten to know and respect already. We had a connection. Maybe I could twist her arm?

David Vess, our school board member, had also become a good friend of mine throughout this process. Fortunately for us, he had a connection with the Fire Department also. David called and asked the question, "Would they be willing to rent that building to us?" The answer, "Not a chance." They already had offers on it and they needed to sell it. The money was necessary for them. Nobody was surprised. Scratch that off the list. Move on to the next possible place.

The next day, I was walking down the hall at school when someone called my name. "Hey Coach, can you take a phone call in the office?" I stepped in to the office and answered the phone. It was Cathy. I remember it like it was yesterday.

"Hey Adam, would you be willing to come and meet with us at our staff meeting and just explain a little bit about what you are doing and what you would use the building for? We might be able to work something out for a better price."

"I will absolutely be there," I said, and I went home and started to get ready for a board meeting the next night. Interestingly enough, our son Drew was in school studying Geographical Information Systems (GIS) at the time. He was in need of something specific to do for a class project. Drew has a lot of talents, but for some reason, I don't know that even he could speak to exactly why, he had chosen to pursue GIS. The timing couldn't have been much better. I seem to say that quite a bit. Anyhow, through some of the statistical and geographical programs that he had access to, Drew was able to pull some information relating to population, poverty levels, etc. Through this information, he came to the conclusion that right in a narrow radius of Sparkman Middle would be the ideal place for community food pantry. He was able to put what we were already experiencing into words with data that supported it. Much credit goes to Drew for building a presentation that I would take to the Fire Department the next evening and for helping me understand all the variables and the obvious conclusion they spoke to.

The following day David Vess and I went to the Harvest Fire Department staff meeting and I presented to them what we were doing, how we were doing it, and why it was important to the children and families of the Harvest community. We sat in that meeting and shared stories with the Fire Department of all the sadness, brokenness, and tragic situations that we have seen the children of Madison County facing, hoping to move their hearts to understand the need for what we are doing. I will never forget hearing the response, as those firefighters, volunteers, began to tell me stories of going into the homes of some of these children in the middle of the night and seeing no food in the house. They shared with me a story of one family whose house they ran a call to...three kids and one can of corn in the pantry. Have you ever walked into a situation expecting to impact someone else and then God flips it around on you when you least expect it? This was that night for me. I left there in shock.

I talked with some of the members of the Fire Department that night. They had a desire to sell the building to meet some of their needs. They pulled me aside before I left and talked about decreasing the price of the building significantly if we were interested. We were...but $100,000 was still going to be pretty tough for us to come by. Cathy talked with me privately and said she felt confident they could get it closer to $80,000. It's pretty humbling to have someone make that kind of offer to you. But we still weren't even close to being able to make that work. My mind began to race from that point. I have always been a problem-solver. How could we raise the money? Is there someone who would loan the money? What would a mortgage look like and how could we be confident we could pay it? At this point, we didn't even have a dime to our name. We weren't taking donations. We were just going out and finding a way to meet the need that was directly in front of us. The prospect of people giving us that kind of money monthly wasn't even on our radar.

We dismissed that night and after a few more days came up with a temporary agreement. The Fire Department graciously offered to let us use the building after they moved to their new location if it hadn't sold yet. The building would remain on the market and we would pay the utility bill each month. This was perfect for us. It would allow us to be able to see if what we were doing was going to be a worthwhile investment for our community in a relatively low-risk way. We were pleased to have the opportunity to see if what we were doing was going to work.

The story of Joseph has always been one of the most amazing stories in all the Bible in my mind. Out of jealousy, his brothers devise a plot to kill him, throw his body in a pit, and say that he was eaten by a wild animal. Can you even imagine? One of his brothers comes to his rescue and encourages the others not to kill him. But then another sees a caravan of Ishmaelites on the way to Egypt and has the bright idea to sell Joseph as a slave, which they agree on for twenty shekels of silver. So here is Joseph, seventeen years old, great-grandson of Abraham, and his brothers sell him as a slave...valuing his life at a mere $220. When he gets to Egypt he is sold again as a slave to one of Pharaoh's officers. Up to this point, a pretty unintriguing story. I would imagine Joseph's brothers felt the same way.

But the next few chapters in the book of Genesis will unfold an incredible story of God's wisdom, love, and providence over the life of Joseph, the bloodline of Abraham, and His ability to write things in the past that will carry enormous weight in the future. God takes Joseph as a slave in Egypt and gives him wisdom, insight, revelation, and raises him up in the house of Pharaoh. Pharaoh, the most powerful man in the world, declares that "the Spirit of God" is with Joseph, and he makes him the highest authority in Egypt, only under himself. Quite a drastic change for the seventeen-year-old whose brothers traded him for a couple hundred bucks, who served as a slave, was thrown into prison, and was treated as a nobody.

And as the story continues to unfold, it will be Joseph's brothers, the ones who sold him into slavery, that will come to Egypt in search of food because of a famine in their homeland. At the point of being reunited, Genesis 41 says of Joseph, "All the world came to Egypt to buy grain from Joseph" (Genesis 41:57 NIV). Pharaoh tells Joseph to send for his family and he will give them the best of the land of Egypt for them to live in. Sure enough, all of Jacob's house makes the journey to Egypt where Joseph is reunited with his family.

There is so much in the story of Joseph that speaks to God's wisdom, love, power, and providence. It is amazing to read all the details of how it unfolds, and He keeps His hand over Joseph even through the darkest times in his life. It is a beautiful message for us as to God's presence at those very same points in our lives. But the story here is that God was writing a script that nobody, not even Joseph, was able to see. Nobody could understand it. Nobody could make sense out of it. The only thing that matters, is that long before that moment that Abraham's family faced death by starvation, God had already used the jealousy of Joseph's brothers and an unjust trip to prison to position Joseph where He needed him to be so that everyone could be provided for. In fact, Joseph would tell his brothers, "You intended to harm me, but God intended it for good, to accomplish what is now being done, the saving of many lives" (Genesis 50:20 NIV).

As time was passing, the Fire Department was bringing together a plan for us to rent their building temporarily. They were finalizing a written agreement with their realtor. On our side, we were just waiting to see what would materialize. Some different discussions had been tossed around. Finally, one night they called and asked if we could set up a meeting. I was at work at Sparkman Middle School when the paperwork was dropped off for me to sign. They had come up with an arrangement for us to pay the money when we were able and had written that in the contract. At this point, the realtor really started pushing Jennifer and I to sign. We were really at a loss as to what to do next. Jennifer and I had no plans to sign those papers and take on that building debt ourselves. Looking back, it was a lack of faith in what God was able to do, but we were definitely walking on unfamiliar ground. We had a long talk that night and decided we just couldn't do it.

I was back at work the next day when I got a phone call from one of the Fire Department Board Members. Seems there was a snag in the process when they were drawing up the contract. The HVFD attorney had a letter on file that was signed back in 1961, by the original families that began the Harvest Volunteer Fire Department. One of those families had donated the land, a handful of guys got together and built the structure, and the Harvest Volunteer Fire Department was born. And as they began serving the Harvest community, these original members laid out in writing that this building was a donation to the Harvest community and that it would forever be in the possession of the Harvest community and used for community purposes, so the building couldn't even be sold! In the event that it was no longer to be used by the community, then the ownership of the building would transfer back to the family of the individual who donated it. This letter was signed by all the families involved and attached to the deed.

That piece of paper changed everything about the arrangements that we were making. About an hour after I received this information, the real estate agent called again to ask if he could bring the papers by the school for me to sign. I told him, "We aren't signing those papers." Just a few days later, we met with the HVFD to draw up a contract for a temporary rental agreement. It was in the middle of this meeting that the HVFD members asked to be dismissed. They stepped outside for about five minutes, re-entered the building, and gave us the news that they had decided to sell the building to us for one dollar! House of the Harvest began, all because of that one piece of paper, signed over fifty years before House of the Harvest was even a thought.

God had been making plans for that piece of land, that building, and for the Harvest community all those years before. Just like when He had moved Joseph to Egypt because He was making plans for His people. The same God who sent Joseph to Egypt, raised him up to second in command to Pharaoh, and gave him charge over all the food in Egypt, that very same God had made a plan for the Harvest community, had some guys put it in writing, and brought up all the people around and put them all in the right place to create the situation we were seeing now. And He showed up at the moment that looked the darkest, the time when everyone thought it just wasn't going to come together.

6

Having No Power

Learning to let God lead has been a major
challenge for me. I have spent most of my life learning a
great deal about God, but not ever learning to experience
God and be in relationship with Him. I never learned that
God was real, alive, and active in my life. I was taught that
God wasn't at work anymore, miracles had ceased, and
that He was watching from above, waiting to see how
good I was or wasn't at living out the book He sent. I am
so grateful that I have been able to see, experience, and
have relationship with the God who is far greater, more
loving, gracious, merciful, and involved! Yes! I am so

thankful that I have learned how He is involved in my life. He desires to be my Father, not my judge. And that has changed my life.

There have been so many moments along the way that have energized my faith and my walk with God here on this Earth. Most of them, a product of me having no idea what I was doing. Jennifer and I never set out to start a food pantry. We never set out to be in the position we are in now. We didn't seek it. We just wanted to meet the need in front of us at the time. The plan was God's and as a result, from the beginning, we have felt like we really didn't know what we were doing. I can confidently say that four years later, we still don't know what we are doing. But God knows exactly what He is doing, and His knowing is way better than anything we could orchestrate, so we try to follow along and just enjoy walking by His Spirit. That is a great challenge too, but one we are committed to.

The greatest part of the whole journey for me has been watching God deliver when we have been unable to do so our ourselves. This has increased my faith, taught me about God, and shown me more than anything I could gain by just reading. These are the moments that we have learned that the God of the Bible is real, active, alive, concerned about my problems, and desires to be involved. And He has solutions that I can't even imagine.

The first year we were open we had no idea what we were doing. I think we have a little better idea now, although there are still moments where it feels like we are on an island. One Wednesday night that first year, we were over at the building trying to get things set up for Saturday morning. All of our pickups had been run, everything we knew was coming in, was already in. Jennifer and I started getting things ready that night, and both of us became increasingly concerned. We normally run anywhere from fifteen to as many as twenty item stations on a Saturday morning. This week we were looking at about eight or nine.

Jennifer looked at me at one point and said, "There is hardly anything in here." I am not usually one to become overwhelmed with a problem in front of me, but this situation proved to be more than I was ready for. Usually, in situations where I am unsure, I can come up with some kind of plan and speak it with enough confidence to get buy in from those around me, but this problem was a little bit bigger than anything I could work up a solution to. In just slightly more than forty-eight hours, there were going to be two hundred plus families outside waiting in line to receive food and we are going to have less than half of what they typically receive when they come in the door.

What we hadn't learned yet, but we were about to, is that God is in control of it all. He knows what is needed where, and how to get it there, and when. He doesn't need me to orchestrate any of it. He doesn't need me, Jennifer or anyone else to be worried about it and stressing about it. In fact, Jesus would say,

> "Therefore I tell you, do not worry about
> your life, what you will eat or drink; or
> about your body, what you will wear. Is
> not life more than food, and the body
> more than clothes? Look at the birds of
> the air; they do not sow or reap or store
> away in barns, and yet your heavenly
> Father feeds them. Are you not much
> more valuable than they? Can any one of
> you by worrying add a single hour to your
> life?

And why do you worry about clothes? See how the flowers of the field grow. They do not labor or spin. Yet I tell you that not even Solomon in all his splendor was dressed like one of these. If that is how God clothes the grass of the field, which is here today and tomorrow is thrown into the fire, will he not much more clothe you—you of little faith?

So do not worry, saying, 'What shall we eat?' or 'What shall we drink?' or 'What shall we wear?' For the pagans run after all these things, and your heavenly Father knows that you need them. But seek first his kingdom and his righteousness, and all these things will be given to you as well. Therefore do not worry about tomorrow, for tomorrow will worry about itself. Each day has enough trouble of its own."

Matthew 6:25-34 NIV

It's just so hard to allow those verses to be real, alive, and active when you are in the moment with your problem. But this was one of those moments where God was about to teach us how alive His Word is, how real He is, how involved and in control He is, and how little He really does want us to be controlled by anxiety over things we can't control. Father, increase our faith!

We stood there, without an answer. Soon to be two hundred families at the door and what are we going to tell them? I had no idea. Jennifer had no idea. It was Jennifer who said, "We just need to pray about it." And for the first time, I think in my entire life, we prayed for God to be the answer from a place of complete helplessness. We asked God to do what only He could do. We pleaded with Him to take this burden and solve it, because we had no way to make it happen. And then we went on our way, still stressed about it. Jesus would have stood right there in the middle of the two of us and said, "You of little faith."

Second Chronicles 20 holds one of my favorite Bible stories of all time. Jehoshaphat was king in Judah at the time. He was one of the good kings that tried to create reform in Judah in the name of the Lord. In 2 Chronicles 20, the armies of the Ammonites, Moabites, and some of the Meunites came together to attack Jehoshaphat and the army of Judah. By the time the king gets the information, these armies are already on the move and closing in. Without hesitation, it seems, Jehoshaphat knows how to respond to this information. He stands up in front of the people at the temple in Jerusalem and prays. Here is the conclusion of that prayer, "...For we have no power to stand against this vast army that is attacking us. We do not know what to do, but our eyes are on You" (2 Chronicles 20:12 NIV).

That's an interesting place to be. The place where you literally have no idea what to do other than put it in God's hands and plead with Him to provide what you need. Interestingly enough, a man in that assembly replies to Jehoshaphat. The man's name is Jahaziel and here is what he has to say, "The Lord says to you: Do not be discouraged because of this vast army. For the battle is not yours, but God's. Tomorrow march down against them...You will not have to fight this battle. Take up your positions, stand firm, and see the deliverance the Lord will give you" (2 Chronicles 20:15-17 NIV). I will let you read how the rest of the story unfolds from 2 Chronicles 20:20-25.

"Early in the morning they left for the Desert of Tekoa. As they set out, Jehoshaphat stood and said, "Listen to me, Judah and people of Jerusalem! Have faith in the Lord your God and you will be upheld; have faith in his prophets and you will be successful." After consulting the people, Jehoshaphat appointed men to sing to the Lord and to praise him for the splendor of his holiness as they went out at the head of the army, saying: "Give thanks to the Lord, for his love endures forever." As they began to sing and praise, the Lord set ambushes against the men of Ammon and Moab and Mount Seir who were invading Judah, and they were defeated. The Ammonites and Moabites rose up against the men from Mount Seir to destroy and annihilate them. After they finished slaughtering the men from Seir, they helped to destroy one another.

When the men of Judah came to the place
that overlooks the desert and looked
toward the vast army, they saw only dead
bodies lying on the ground; no one had
escaped. So Jehoshaphat and his men went
to carry off their plunder, and they found
among them a great amount of equipment
and clothing and also articles of value—
more than they could take away. There was
so much plunder that it took three days to
collect it."

2 Chronicles 20:20-25 NIV

I love this story! It has become a go-to in the
moments when I just don't have an answer. Can you
imagine being overcome with fear as you prepare to face
an army that overwhelms yours in just a matter of hours? I
can't even put myself in the position to understand what
that would feel like. But I can relate to facing problems
that I can't possibly have the answer to, nobody I know
has the answer to, and they are pressing in on me right
now. And just at this moment, Jehoshaphat knows exactly
where to turn and he does just that.

Maybe he was expecting God to answer? Maybe he was confident that God would answer? His faith was way bigger than a mustard seed in this moment. Sometimes I wonder how much smaller mine is than a mustard seed. But whatever the case, God flips all three of those armies against each other, they all destroy each other, and the Israelites come in without lifting a finger and spend three days gathering the spoils.

Can it get any better than that? What an incredible story! How great is our God! Every time I read this story, I pray for God to increase my faith, destroy my unbelief and help me to live in this reality that He has the answer when I don't. He has had the answer all along and He is just waiting for me to realize how to walk with Him in His way instead of trying to plead with Him to walk with me in my way.

Jennifer and I both had grown up in church. My parents were very religious, loved God and sought to honor Him with their lives, and had taught us to do the same. I had learned how to go to church, learned the stories of scripture, learned to try to live out the fruit of the Spirit. But, I never learned how to pray, at least not with an expectation. I mean I learned how to thank God for meals, mention the people I knew who were sick, and ask God to forgive my sins. I learned to pray on the surface level. But this was different. This was praying from a place of complete desperation, a place of true helplessness. This is walking by faith. This is knowing God, not knowing about God. This is putting the words of the Bible into action in my life, not just being able to tell you what it says and where to find it. This was a new way of living, and only God could teach us how to walk in it.

For two days, Jennifer and I prayed. This was one of those 2 Chronicles 20 moments. But I wasn't really good at recognizing those moments in my life yet. We were desperate. We woke up Thursday morning and started getting ready for work. I sat down in the bathroom floor at 5:00 AM to talk with her as she put on her makeup, our morning ritual. And we made a commitment to each other that we would both keep praying about it over the next couple of days and we went on to work.

For two days my phone rang. I think I got more phone calls and emails about people wanting to donate food than I have ever gotten in any two day span since. It was unbelievable! My phone rang more than it does at Thanksgiving and Christmas. In fact, there was so much food that came in, it was still coming in Saturday morning minutes before we opened. I remember at one point, I had to climb to the top shelf that we rarely used to find somewhere to put more. As a sat on the top shelf, stacking up boxes, another person came in and said, "Someone is here to drop-off donations." I couldn't do anything but laugh.

We were pulling out tables that we hadn't used in months to keep food off the floors. We had filled the shelves all the way to the top. Dennison Farms sent nine hundred pounds of squash. A lady who lived in South Huntsville called and donated a truck load of food that she normally sent to another pantry, but she was unable to get in touch with anyone there. Words can't even express what it was like to watch that scene unfold from our perspective. There were so many things going on, that we couldn't even begin to wrap our minds around it. It was a story that had to be told!

Here are just a couple of stories from that week that have to be shared. Friday I was standing in the gym at Sparkman Middle, where I was one of the PE teachers alongside Brian Gunnels. Brian was asking me about the kind of food we give out at House of the Harvest. I said something about not having any meat at the moment, when my phone rang. It was a friend of ours who wishes to remain anonymous. She called and asked if I could meet her at HOH because she was bringing two hundred packages of hot dogs for us to give out.

On Wednesday of that week, I had told Fran that I was coming to pick up a load of cereal for us that afternoon and my schedule just got turned upside down. I had planned to be there at 2:00 and communicated that to her, but I didn't actually make it until around 6:00. As a result she had given away our cereal because she thought I had already come and picked up what we needed. You can't even imagine how hard I was kicking myself for that. Saturday morning someone pulls up from Ford's Chapel United Methodist Church, us unaware they were coming, with over two hundred boxes of cereal to donate.

I can't even begin to speak of all the private donations that came in that day. The whole community had played a part. It was incredible to see how God had orchestrated it all.

We broke two tables that morning. I remember standing at the road just watching as we opened the doors and food was falling everywhere. It was like it couldn't be contained by the building. I don't know that we have ever had as much food in there at one time as we did that morning for about thirty minutes. It was truly incredible.

It's funny how God gives us small things to share and moments to enjoy. And He can send the right person at the right time with the right words. As I stood at the road watching in awe, God sent me one of those moments. Tony Pitsinos walks up behind me. Tony and his wife Rachel go to church with us at the Light. Tony has a way of being the right person, at the right time, with the right words in my life. Today was no different. I replayed the story from Wednesday to Saturday. Tony replied, "Empty tables on Wednesday and breaking tables on Saturday. It's like the feeding of the 5,000."

Yes it is, Tony. Yes it is. It's exactly like that. Father, teach me to be that dependent on You for everything in my life. Increase my faith in the name of Jesus. Amen.

7

As We Are

God has increased my faith in so many ways since House of the Harvest began. I really have been fortunate to go through a huge transformation in my thinking, my faith, and my walk with Him. One of the greatest things I have been able to experience is learning how to spend time with God and letting Him teach me what He desires for me to learn. Every now and then during my prayer time, I will just ask God if there is something He wants to share with me. As I sit in solitude, often times God will send me a word to study or even a specific Bible story or text.

One Wednesday morning, I was praying this prayer when the Spirit of God led me to James 5. I turned over to James 5 and began to read. When I do this, I like to read primarily for anything that I feel really drawn to and then I will begin to study that text deeper. This morning, as I read from James 5, I was particularly drawn to verses 16 through 18.

> "The prayer of a righteous person is powerful and effective. Elijah was a human being, even as we are. He prayed earnestly that it would not rain, and it did not rain on the land for three and a half years. Again he prayed, and the heavens gave rain, and the earth produced its crops."

James 5:16-18 NIV

I sat down with my journal and began to copy down those verses. I prayed for the kind of faith that Elijah had. Faith that would believe enough to even ask God to stop the rain. I prayed for a prayer life that was bold and powerful and effective. Even as I write this, more than a year later, I desire for my prayer life to look more like this on a consistent basis. It's amazing how God will honor prayers that are about us learning to be like Him, think like Him, understand life like Him. Some of my greatest moments with God have grown out of asking Him to teach me more about Him, the way He thinks, the way He sees life. It's amazing how this world and all that comes with it can distract me from this type of intentional focus in my prayer life.

I wrote those verses down on a note card that day and carried them with me. This is my practice sometimes when I feel that God's Spirit has led me to a particular text but I am not sure exactly why or what God intends for me to get from it. Sometimes after I carry that text for a few hours or even days and have more time to study it, or even through conversations with other people, God will open my understanding of that passage. At this point, I will gain understanding of what it was that He desired for me to see and understand.

I carried these verses with me for two days. Friday morning before school I had to go pick up bread at Publix. Our normal pickup person was unable to run this particular week. Publix pickup runs at 7:00 AM when they open and then I had to be at school, in class at 8:00. It takes about twenty minutes to get the Publix items to the car, another ten or so to drive them out to House of the Harvest, a few minutes to unload, and then head to work. I knew I was going to be pushing it for time, but I could make it if everything went smooth.

I got in the truck and started on my way to Publix. It rained from the time I left our house all the way there. The whole way I am thinking, "Maybe it won't be raining when I get to Harvest." Wishful thinking it turns out. I pull in to Publix in Harvest, still raining. Here is the bigger problem....I can't transport bread and bakery items in my truck from Harvest in the rain. It will be ruined. We need that bread Saturday morning. I can't wait for the rain to stop. I have to be at work in an hour and traffic will be terrible in twenty minutes. Maybe I could call someone else to pick up the bread? Or maybe wait it out and call someone to cover my class? Anxiety is taking over. I got to have the bread and bakery. I got to get to work. Who can I depend on? Who can I call?

Someone came to my aid. Although not necessarily who I thought it would be. Sitting in that parking lot at Harvest Publix, the Holy Spirit speaks to my heart. "Remember those verses you have been carrying around." Ha. I knew it would be revealed in time. I do remember. And I start to pray. "God, I know you focused my heart on these verses two days ago. So I feel like you are already going to do this. Even though I have never done this before. Your word says Elijah was a human just like me and You answered his prayers. Right now I really need this rain to stop so I can get this bread delivered and get to work. If You could do that for me right now, I would really appreciate it."

In John 14 Jesus told His disciples that a Helper would come. He told them that that Helper, the Holy Spirit, sent from the Father, would teach them all things and bring to their remembrance all that He had said. He was my Helper on this particular day. I got out of my truck that morning and walked into Publix just a few minutes after 7:00 AM. The rain had stopped. I loaded the entire bed of the truck with bread and bakery items to give to the needy at House of the Harvest Saturday morning. The rain remained stopped. I drove out to House of the Harvest, pulled in and started to unload bread. I took the last tub of bread out of the back of my truck and started walking toward the door. By the time I dropped it on the table, turned around, cut the lights out and checked to make sure the door was locked, it had started to pour down rain.

The Holy Spirit made the promise all those years ago through the pen of James. Elijah was a human, even as we are. He served a God who answered prayers. The God of the Bible. Fortunately for us, "He is the same yesterday, today, and forever" (Hebrews 13:8 NIV). Fortunately for us, He loves us just the same as He did Elijah, James, or anyone else. And fortunately for us, Jesus spoke the truth when He said He would send a Helper, the Holy Spirit who would "teach you all things and will remind you of everything I have said to you" (John 14:26 NIV). I wouldn't want to live my life without Him. The bread would be wet and I would be late for work.

Thank You, Father, for answering the prayers of men and women just like us. Thank You for teaching us more about You and the way You love us. Teach us to understand more. Increase our faith in the name of Jesus. Amen.

8

Found

It was the Saturday before Christmas, 2017. The Saturday before Christmas is always hectic. There are people everywhere. It's been a process for me learning how to handle the whole thing. When we first started I would be so wound up in anticipation of how things were going to go, what might happen, and so on. It's funny how your mind can make a "mountain out of a molehill" when you don't know what you are dealing with. It's also funny how experience brings wisdom and that allows you to be able to remain calm in those situations. I think Christmas 2017 was probably the first time that I was really able to enjoy the "controlled chaos" of the Holidays at House of the Harvest. I had no idea what God had in store.

Everything was going pretty smooth that morning. We had a big crowd. The building was full inside with helpers and outside with families. We were giving out food as normal, gifts for the children, and Christmas meals for Monday. As things were moving along, I noticed a lady coming through the line that I hadn't seen before. She was walking the line with tears in her eyes the entire time. As she came toward the end, she was overwhelmed with emotions. I had to ask her what was going on. She began to unfold her story.

Earlier that morning, she sat in her car at the Mapco across the street. She held in her hand the last dollar she had to her name. She had been through three surgeries in the last year, lost her job as a result of the amount of work she had missed, been unable to find a job on account of her age and health, and was down to one dollar. One dollar that she planned to spend on a cup of coffee that morning as she contemplated ending her life that day. Two days before Christmas. While the world is hustling to figure out last minute gifts and complaining about the chaos that is Christmas shopping, there is this lady out there, and several more just like her, so stripped of joy and hope that the Christmas season could be enough to push them to the point of suicide.

And reflecting back on that, and thinking about Jesus and His heart for everyone, regardless of my perception, it makes me ask myself this question, "Where would He be in that moment?" The entire intent of the whole season is to bring honor and glory to our Savior and how easily we can lose focus of Him and where He would be. Matthew (25:31-46) said it better than I ever could...

> "When the Son of Man comes in his glory, and all the angels with him, he will sit on his glorious throne. All the nations will be gathered before him, and he will separate the people one from another as a shepherd separates the sheep from the goats. He will put the sheep on his right and the goats on his left.
>
> Then the King will say to those on his right, 'Come, you who are blessed by my Father; take your inheritance, the kingdom prepared

for you since the creation of the world. For I was hungry and you gave me something to eat, I was thirsty and you gave me something to drink, I was a stranger and you invited me in, I needed clothes and you clothed me, I was sick and you looked after me, I was in prison and you came to visit me.'

Then the righteous will answer him, 'Lord, when did we see you hungry and feed you, or thirsty and give you something to drink? When did we see you a stranger and invite you in, or needing clothes and clothe you? When did we see you sick or in prison and go to visit you?'

The King will reply, 'Truly I tell you, whatever you did for one of the least of these brothers and sisters of mine, you did for me.'

Then he will say to those on his left, 'Depart from me, you who are cursed, into the eternal fire prepared for the devil and his angels. For I was hungry and you gave me nothing to eat, I was thirsty and you gave me nothing to drink, I was a stranger and you did not invite me in, I needed clothes and you did not clothe me, I was sick and in prison and you did not look after me.'

They also will answer, 'Lord, when did we see you hungry or thirsty or a stranger or needing clothes or sick or in prison, and did not help you?

He will reply, 'Truly I tell you, whatever you did not do for one of the least of these, you did not do for me.'

Then they will go away to eternal punishment, but the righteous to eternal life."

Matthew 25:31-46 NIV

For me, Christmas is my favorite time of the year. I love the music, the lights, the decorations, the movies, and especially the spirit. I love the fact that it causes people to stop and focus some of their attention on Jesus the Messiah, the Savior. But I love the fact that, in this text, Matthew chooses to call Him the King. I think it's easy for our minds to be drawn to Jesus the Savior, but we struggle with Jesus the King. Even during Christmas. We celebrate the Savior! Amen. All glory and praise to the Lamb that was slain! If our King were physically here today, He would be about His Father's business of seeking the lost, the broken, the hungry and thirsty.

Back to my story, she begins to unfold the events of that morning for me as she sits at Mapco, a dollar to her name and ready to be done with all of it. In her car, in the Mapco parking lot, she cries until she can cry no more, gathers herself enough to go inside the store. As she walks in the store, the cashier asks her, "Baby, what is wrong?" Have you ever asked that question to a complete stranger, only to have them unload everything on you? This was one of those moments. One of those Holy Spirit prompted moments. One of those moments where the King smiles down on His little sheep behind the register at the Harvest, Alabama Mapco.

And the lady unloads. "I have no money. I have no food. I have nothing. I am just so tired and I can't even feed my children for Christmas." Hopeless. Lost. Broken. And the sheep says, "I am so sorry sweetheart. Can you go to the place across the street?"

Way back in the book of Genesis, chapter 12, Abraham was seventy-five years old. God made a promise to Abraham, at the age of seventy-five, that He would bless all nations of the earth through him. What an amazing promise that must have been to receive from the God of the universe! Over the next twenty-five years, as Abraham's wife Sarah remained barren, they tried every way to figure out how to make this promise come true. In chapter fifteen, Abraham tries to take a servant of his own house to be his heir. God responds and says, "No, a son who will be your own flesh and blood. Not this boy." In chapter sixteen, Sarah comes up with a plan for Abraham to have a child with her Egyptian slave, Hagar, saying, "The Lord has kept me from having children. Perhaps I can build a family through her" (Genesis 16:2 NIV).

Shortly after, Hagar becomes pregnant and Sarah begins to despise her. As a result, Sarah starts to mistreat Hagar to the point that Hagar runs from her. Can you even imagine what Hagar felt like at this point? An Egyptian slave, mistreated by the family that has provided for her and sustained her existence. Now she has run from them to get away. She is pregnant, not by choice, but by following orders from the man and woman who owned her and then decided they didn't want her or her baby around after they decided that she was going to carry the baby that he was the father of! If there is anything worse than being a slave, I would say it would have to be Hagar's situation. I can't even imagine what she felt like.

And now, on top of all that...what is she going to eat? How will she provide for this baby? How is she going to survive? Where will she go? One thing I have learned from House of the Harvest is that sometimes people stay in awful situations because the questions on the other side are just too overwhelming. They can't be answered. Here is Hagar, pregnant, and with nothing but a list of questions that she can't answer.

And at the moment of Hagar's misery, she finds hope in a place of hopelessness, by a spring in the desert the Bible says. The angel of the Lord found her. Funny how He has a way of doing that. The angel says to Hagar, "Where are you going?" (Genesis 16:8 NIV). Hagar begins to explain.

The angel says, "Go back to your mistress and submit to her. I will increase your descendants so much that they will be too numerous to count...You are now pregnant and you will give birth to a son. You shall name him Ishmael, for the Lord has heard of your misery" (Genesis 16:9-11 NIV). The name Ishmael in Hebrew means, "God will hear."

How awesome is that? In the moment of despair, when Hagar has no answers, God sends an angel to her with a message, "I hear you in your misery. I have heard everything. I feel your pain. You can do this. I am with you. That son you carry is from Me and your descendants will be numerous!" A message from God at the moment of brokenness, despair, hopelessness. And doesn't God have a way of sending messages of joy, hope, and triumph? I love that story.

Back to Harvest MAPCO, 2017. "What's across the street?" the lady asks. The sheep replies, "I'm not really sure but it's one of those places that will give you food." Over the years, I have learned that different people say that with different intent behind it. This day, it was a message from the angel of the Lord.

That lady came across the street that morning. She walked in the front door at House of the Harvest and found a Christmas meal to enjoy with her children. She found bread, lots of bread...more bread than she could eat in a week. She found more tears. She only thought she had cried them all. She found Lisa Parvin, another sheep, angel, whichever you prefer. She found prayer. Later she told me that three people prayed with her that morning. Maybe God knew she needed a little extra. She found hope. Enough hope to help her gather herself, get back up, and keep moving. Over the next couple of weeks that same lady found a job...a good job, a manager job. And above it all, she found Jesus. She was baptized just over a month later.

In the Bible, God would often change people's names to mean something different when they came to know Him. He changed Abram's name to Abraham, Sarai's to Sarah. He changed Saul's name to Paul. Jesus changed Simon's name to Peter. Sometimes I think that God still changes our names in Heaven. Can you imagine God the Father and Jesus talking about you the sheep, how much They love you, how proud They are of you and calling you by the name They have designated for you? Not the name that people on earth call you that carries your past mistakes and failures that everyone wants to remember you by. Not the name that people use when they talk of your negative qualities and shortcomings. But the name that sums you up perfectly in the eyes of the Father. The name that describes your best characteristics, those that God breathed into you in your mother's womb,

and nurtured in you through orchestrated life experiences.
I wonder if God changed our friend's name that morning
to something like Ishmael, "I have heard your misery."

9

The 7:00 AM Struggle

Seven A.M. on a Saturday morning is early to most of us. It can be a struggle to get up after a long week. Especially to get up, get ready, and come to do volunteer work. That is why Jennifer and I try to be so grateful and gracious to everyone that comes to help. God never fails to move enough hearts to be there on a Saturday. It always comes together like it should. Most Saturdays, we have people show up late and can't find a spot to help. Sometimes they hang around, sometimes they don't. Either way is fine. God works in all of it.

Kevin and Kristie Smith have been friends of ours for a long time. Their son Zach was friends with Drew growing up. Kevin really has a special way with young men. He has been a huge blessing to Drew. Kristie, a nurse, was there in the delivery room when Ty was born. They are two of our closest friends and they come to House of the Harvest pretty frequently. One day Kevin and Kristi gave us a peek into their "7:00 AM struggle."

Kevin and Kristie had gotten up that morning with not a whole lot going on. By his own admission, Kevin had planned to "post up" on the couch and watch football that day...all day. We males are guilty of that from time to time. Kristie came in the living room and said, "I think I am going to go to House of the Harvest this morning." Kevin blew it off. The "7:00 AM struggle" is real. As a result, Kristie dismissed the idea herself.

A little time went by. She felt nudged. And nudged again. And again. This time she moved. She tells Kevin, "I am going. You can stay home if you want." Of course, Kevin joins. They were late that morning. Really late. Not a whole lot to do. Unless of course, something or Someone greater called you to be there.

There is a book in the Bible by the name of Esther. It's a short book. You can read it pretty quickly. It's an interesting book. God is not even mentioned in it. In fact, it is one of only two books in the Bible where God is not mentioned at all. The theme of the book is His unseen involvement in the world. He is unseen but involved in the book of Esther. Highly involved. John Wesley described it like this, "The name of God is not found in this book: but the finger of God is, directing so many minute events for the deliverance of His people."

Esther was a Jew. At the time they were in Exile. Xerxes the Great was King in Persia. He was known for hosting banquets of celebration and drinking...lots of drinking. His wife, Queen Vashti, was a beautiful woman. When King Xerxes and his officials had gotten very drunk, he would call for Vashti to come into their presence so he could "display her beauty." On this particular occasion, it was the seventh day of Xerxes' drunkenness when he called for his queen. She refused.

King Xerxes had to make a statement to the women of the world. This would clearly not be tolerated. The Queen would not be allowed to come into his presence ever again. She would be replaced. The King's men begin a search to bring a new Queen into the castle. They would search all the land for the most beautiful young women, bring them to the castle, give them beauty treatments for a year and then bring them before the king and he would choose his new queen.

It was Esther, unknowingly a Jew, who the King would choose to be his new queen. And it was through this act, God raising her up at this moment, that Esther would be able to reveal the plot of Haman, the king's second in charge, to destroy the Jews. Haman was angered by Mordecai, Esther's cousin, who refused to bow down and worship him at the city gate. Haman became so angry at Mordecai that he calculated a plan to destroy all the Jews because they "keep themselves separate and do not obey the king's laws" (Esther 3:8 NIV).

Esther becomes the queen. She gains favor in the king's eyes. And because of her position, Esther is able to save God's people in the presence of the king and even have the Jews elevated in the eyes of King Xerxes. It's an inspiring story of God's providence, and how He works in unseen ways toward His ends for His children. There is so much mystery to the God of the Bible. There is so much our human minds can't grasp or even begin to understand. But what we can see and clearly embrace is that the God of the Bible works through the thoughts, intents, emotions, and plans of man to bring us to Him.

Kevin and Kristie entered that morning just in time. Mid-way through the line, a woman fell out on the ground. I was outside when people started hollering for me. As I entered the room, she was on the floor, someone was already calling 911, and a couple of people were trying to tend to her. Kristie had the presence of mind to notice the young lady had been eating. She was a diabetic. Kristie swept her mouth to get out the granola bar she was eating, got her the attention that she needed, and brought her back to consciousness. The ambulance came and picked the young lady up and took her to the hospital. By the time it arrived, she was conscious, aware, and able to get herself onto the stretcher. Kristie had been there right by her side, aiding her back to health.

It was God that moved Kristie to be present that morning. It wasn't that there wasn't anyone else present that knew what to do. We had other people with the proper training that acted on the woman's behalf. But it was Kristie's wisdom to intervene in the situation with calmness, clarity, and the proper training that rescued that young lady in that moment. Kristie Smith was that young lady's Esther. God knew she would need Kristie to be there, and He tugged her heart to bring her. He orchestrated it from start to finish. It's miraculous. It's divine intervention. It's a display of His love toward His children. And it's a blessing to be able to recognize it, live in it, and share it.

10

When You Give a Banquet

Fran was really the first one to cast a vision for us to serve breakfast in the kitchen area at House of the Harvest. She saw it the first time she walked in the building. We always had a plan to be able to do it one day, but the kitchen we had at House of the Harvest wasn't cut out to do much. It had an old gas stove that had seen better days, a refrigerator and that was it. On top of that we had some issues in the kitchen that had to be addressed when the time was right. The cabinets had to be torn out under the sink where they were rotting from water damage. The roof above the kitchen had leaked several years ago and all that sheetrock was turning brown and beginning to crumble. It definitely needed some TLC.

It was almost two years into House of the Harvest when Rick Wilkinson approached me about serving breakfast outside. We set-up a table outside for him and he started serving quesadillas every Saturday morning off a griddle. Rick was cooking over two hundred quesadillas, bacon, sausage, and whatever else he was inclined to serve, all out of his own pocket. We had hoped to start cooking breakfast inside at some point, but we just didn't have the capability to do it very well yet and we needed to bring the kitchen mess together. It wouldn't take long.

God has an interesting way of bringing the right people together at the right time. I have been blessed to watch Him do that over and over again. At a time when I was in pretty desperate need for some help from a driving perspective, God delivered exactly what we needed. Don Sadler, my father-in-law, retired from Sharp Communication, probably a little earlier than he had intended due to some unforeseen circumstances. It wasn't necessarily in his plans, but to some degree, I think it was reward from God for a career of work that served other people well. Don has a heart of gold, loves people, and would literally "do anything for anyone." His retirement was a huge blessing to House of the Harvest. I think it has brought him joy also, joy that working would not have.

About the same time, Wendell Waite retired from his work. I have known Wendell for several years. He was looking for some things to do in his newly found "spare time." And we had plenty. I am not sure what our initial connection with Wendell was. I would guess it was probably Sheila Cooper and Monrovia Church of Christ. Wendell came along at just the right time, with the right Spirit, and the willingness to help out.

It was a typical Saturday morning when Wendell, Jennifer, and Brad Minor all started developing a vision for breakfast on the inside. It all came together so naturally, as things tend to when the Spirit of God is involved. Before long, we would be cooking breakfast for over two hundred people every Saturday morning in addition to giving out the groceries that we give to our families. Every Saturday morning, anyone in the community can come and eat a hot breakfast and enjoy a time of fellowship in our kitchen. And every Saturday morning anyone in the community can come in the front door at House of the Harvest to pick up groceries they need for their family for that week.

Those first few months of Saturdays were a challenge. But God put the right people in place to make

Saturday morning breakfast what it needed to be. Wendell ended up managing the breakfast end of House of the Harvest and bringing along Lin Brittain and Jim Ikard to help him. Those three make a phenomenal team. They are faithful to what God is doing and doing it God's way. It really is a blessing to work with all three of them.

We still weren't equipped to do what we were doing in that small kitchen. It was a sight to see all those Walmart griddles plugged in all over the place and the breakers in the kitchen tripping every 15 minutes or so. Kudos to our breakfast staff for solving problems and making it work. We burned through some electric griddles. God always provides for the need when His work is being done. In keeping with that, it wasn't long before the right people came along with the desire to make our kitchen be what it needed to be. We had someone offer the needed donations to make the repairs that needed to be made and to make the necessary upgrades to bring us up to efficiency.

Today, breakfast at House of the Harvest is a sight to see. You can walk in the kitchen any time after 6:30 in the morning and hear joy and laughter. Jennifer loves it because of that. Just like a mother. It is a tremendous blessing to be able to provide community. Time spent together creates relationship, which sparks love and respect. Since breakfast started at House of the Harvest, there has been a different "spirit in the air." People always tell me how gracious and kind our families are.

Just last week, Kevin Smith came out with his men's study group to cook and serve with our breakfast team. He shared with me that people were coming back in to tell him, "Thank you" for their time cooking that morning. Paul said it like this, "And let the peace of Christ rule in your hearts, to which indeed you were called in one body; and be thankful" (Colossians 3:15 NIV). Where gratitude exists, there is community. When we appreciate, value, and respect one another there is peace. Amen.

God continues to provide in the places where His Spirit is working. You can see evidence of it all around you. We have certainly seen it firsthand at House of the Harvest. We have donors that pay for breakfast every month because they believe in what is being done. Here are the wife's words to describe her passion for our breakfast ministry, "It creates family and community. It provides the community with an opportunity to have relationship with each other and that is exactly what people need. The husband's motivation...the words of Jesus in Luke 14...

"Then Jesus said to his host, "When you give a luncheon or dinner, do not invite your friends, your brothers or sisters, your relatives, or your rich neighbors; if you do, they may invite you back and so you will be repaid. But when you give a banquet, invite the poor, the crippled, the lame, the blind, and you will be blessed. Although they cannot repay you, you will be repaid at the resurrection of the righteous."

Luke 14:12-14 NIV

Over two hundred people eat a free breakfast every Saturday morning because of these words, the gracious hearts of this couple, the volunteers that get up at 5:00 AM to cook, and countless others who have helped with cooking, cleaning, etc. It's a thing of beauty and a blessing to everyone involved. There is something special about doing something for someone that can never repay you. Jesus was onto something when He said that 2,000 years ago. Matter of fact, I like to think that if Jesus were around today, He would be in Harvest, Alabama having breakfast at House of the Harvest on Saturday mornings.

11

Community

One of the most humbling things about running House of the Harvest, is seeing firsthand how much help we receive from the whole community. It is amazing to come in on a Saturday morning and have fifty or sixty, sometimes more people there to volunteer. It is incredible to watch people come in late and not be able to find a place to help because so many people are there to offer their time and energy. The truth is we couldn't do it without all the people that help us get all the work done.

We have multiple Publix pick-ups each week that are handled by Lisa Parvin, Sheila Cooper, Wanda Tucker, Betty Black, Marsha Brock, Willadean Powers and others that fill in from time to time. We have Halsey pickups and Manna House pickups that are handled by Don Sadler (my father-in-law), Wendell Waite, Brad Minor and his son Lawson, Brian Privett and the Light church, Terry Nichols and Lindsay Lane East Baptist Church, Shalunda Sherrod and the students of Oakwood University. We get help on a regular basis from Spencer and Heather Johnson, Rick Nobles, Coaches Andy Blackston and Grant Reynolds and the students of Madison Academy and countless other people who have helped us from time to time. It really is an honor for Jennifer and I to preside over all that has to be managed and the logistics that have to be organized to make House of the Harvest a reality for our community. God is so faithful to provide the food, the volunteers, the finances and everything that has to be done to make it happen.

It is impossible for us to say "thank you" enough for all the help that we get in bringing it all together. Jennifer and I both work full time in demanding jobs. She serves as an elementary school counselor, as well as the coordinator for LEAP Academy, a non-profit summer leadership academy for at-risk students. I am in my first year serving as an elementary assistant principal at a Title I school. I am asked quite frequently, "How do you have the time to do it?" The answer is that we don't have the time, but praise be to God, we do have the people. We could never do it alone. Even back in the days when we first started delivering to families out of Sparkman Middle, we couldn't have done it without our church, the Light, committing to being there every week to pack and deliver those boxes. Their faithfulness to that mission was God's test to see if we would meet the challenge. We are forever grateful to the Light for seeing that through.

I think all of this describes what I love most about House of the Harvest. It's community in action. There are so many people that contribute to the overall working of our organization. It's like an iceberg. There is so much happening under the surface to prepare for a Saturday morning when everyone comes in to put it all together. It really is a blessing to watch. We have several committed regular volunteers each week. Wendell Waite, Lin Brittain, and Jim Ikard are handling breakfast during the week, getting things ready, purchasing, picking up, and coordinating it all for Saturday morning. They have several individuals, families, men's groups, etc. that come in and work on a weekly rotation.

We have had a faithful group since the beginning that manages our food distribution each week. Sheila Cooper and Shalunda Sherrod do an outstanding job at the door. We are blessed to have committed couples that come and work together just about every week: Jeff and Lisa Burgess, Hal and Yvonne Espy, Spencer and Heather Johnson, Ben and Rachel Lowery, David and Tammy Mitchell, and Lisa and Pete Parvin. Jennifer's parents, Don and Molly Sadler, are always willing to do anything, including cleaning the bathrooms each week. And several other individuals that are so willing to do anything that needs to be done for House of the Harvest: Willadean Powers, Don Turney, Ruth Harris, Terri Pennington, Terry Nichols. Without any of these people, it would be impossible for Saturday mornings to happen effectively and efficiently.

On top of all the things that these people do, we couldn't even begin to name all the local churches, schools, farmers, and businesses that participate in our mission. It is such an honor to be a part of a community that is working to love, care, and provide for its' own community. House of the Harvest is a unique place because of this. It is hard to find places any longer where community reigns. It is difficult to find places where people are thinking about others. It's hard to find in our places of employment. Unfortunately, it's becoming increasingly harder to find even in our churches and our families. To me, that is the greatest blessing. Being a part of a community that works together, thrives together, succeeds and fails together is greater than anything I could ever accomplish on my own. We have a phenomenal team at House of the Harvest. It's the best team I have ever coached and it has been a huge blessing.

Our culture has a hard time understanding community. We live in a "me" world. We are taught from a young age that we can be and do anything that we want to. We are taught by our culture to be independent, self-promoting, self-serving, and self-reliant. We learn from our culture that some people have because they have worked and earned, and other people do not because they have been irresponsible and are undeserving. While there is truth in these statements, they aren't the rule. We have learned this from House of the Harvest. Some people are doing the best they can with what they have been given and our community should be proud that they are willing to do what they do. The difference to be able to see and understand...is thinking in terms of "we" instead of "me."

Learning to think as "we" instead of "me" is the key to us accomplishing things that are bigger than ourselves. Jesus said, "You are the light of the world." Our western mindset causes us to read this verse on a personal level. I think the following verse is the key to helping us see that His words were more focused on the community of believers. "A city set on a hill cannot be hidden." Not a person set on a hill. Not if you go stand on a hill. All of us, together, on a hill, cannot be hidden. It's a statement of community. Team. Togetherness. Everyone moving in a common, unified direction.

Jesus was the best at this. He would always focus on the whole over the part. In fact He told His disciples in Luke 14, "For all those who exalt themselves will be humbled, and those who humble themselves will be exalted" (Luke 14:11 NIV). The truth is that He loved so much, He valued others more than His own life. That was evident in the moment of His greatest glory...at the cross. Jesus spent His entire life thinking about the group over Himself. He was the most humble servant of all. Thinking from "we" wasn't a challenge for Him like it is for us.

The picture of a community would be a place where everyone is valued, loved, and respected. It doesn't matter who you are, what role(s) you play, where you come from, or any other factor. You are a member of the community. You are on the team. You are as valuable as any other. And you have a valuable contribution to make to the accomplishment of the whole. For Jesus, the priority was the success of the people, not the success of Himself.

Had His own success been His priority, I think He would have done things much differently. In fact, His clash with the Jewish leaders was based on a difference in priorities. The Jewish leaders thought from the "me" mindset, while Jesus thought from the "we" mindset. Instant conflict.

Read through the gospels and notice how much Jesus preached about the "Kingdom." The kingdom was a community. He didn't preach to people to about personal salvation, although He came to seek and save the lost. His mindset was toward the community of God, the Kingdom. Jesus came to proclaim what God was doing on the earth and to redeem a community of people, a "we" not a "me." He is the King, appointed by God, to lead the community. Our King rules over His community by doing everything upside down compared to the world's traditions. In ancient times, people brought gifts to the King. As our King, Jesus brings gifts to us instead of us bringing gifts to Him. He showers us with love, grace, and mercy. He is the giver of every good and perfect gift. Our King gave His life for the Kingdom, the community. What other king has been willing to die that the community could benefit? Paul wrote about our King in Philippians 2…

Therefore if you have any encouragement from being united with Christ, if any comfort from his love, if any common sharing in the Spirit, if any tenderness and compassion, then make my joy complete by being like-minded, having the same love, being one in spirit and of one mind. Do nothing out of selfish ambition or vain conceit. Rather, in humility value others above yourselves, not looking to your own interests but each of you to the interests of the others. In your relationships with one another, have the same mindset as Christ Jesus:

Who, being in very nature God, did not consider equality with God something to be used to his own advantage; rather, he made himself nothing by taking the very nature of a servant, being made in human likeness. And being found in appearance as a man, he humbled himself by becoming obedient to death—even death on a cross! Therefore God exalted him to

the highest place and gave him the
name that is above every name, that at
the name of Jesus every knee should
bow, in heaven and on earth and under
the earth, and every tongue
acknowledge that Jesus Christ is Lord,
to the glory of God the Father.

Philippians 2:1-11 NIV

Jesus is the ultimate example of the strong reaching down to care for the weak. He is the epitome of loving others that aren't like you, can't do anything for you, and don't add any value to you from a physical standpoint. He is community. He is sacrifice. He is love. He is the greatest "we" thinker of all time. When Paul said, "Be imitators of me, just as I am of Christ" (1 Corinthians 11:1 NASB), I think this is exactly what he was talking about.

12

God-Sized

God is as big as we let Him be. Or maybe, I should say, God is as big as we believe Him to be. My favorite Bible verse used to be Philippians 3:14, "I press on toward the goal for the prize of the upward call of God in Christ Jesus" (NASB). It symbolized what I believed in most at that point in my spiritual journey, what I was doing and how I was working. Looking back, I don't think that was Paul's intent. In fact, I know it wasn't Paul's intent. Paul was enduring...shipwrecks, beatings, being outcast from his society, prison, you name it...Paul dealt with it on account of Jesus. And he pressed on. And said, "by grace you have been saved through faith; and that, not of yourselves, it is the gift of God" (Ephesians 2:8 NASB).

Isn't it funny how even our favorite scriptures are self-centered. "I can do all things through Him who strengthens me" (Philippians 4:13 NASB). Or, "For I know the plans I have for you," declares the LORD, "plans to prosper you and not to harm you, plans to give you hope and a future" (Jeremiah 29:11 NIV). We get so wrapped up in our own lives. A kingdom perspective is hard to achieve in the world we live in.

The greatest lesson I have learned from experiencing God through House of the Harvest is to focus outside myself. What He is doing in the world is much, much bigger than Adam Walker. It's much, much bigger than House of the Harvest. It's much, much bigger than the sum total of all that my life encompasses or could ever encompass. And His greatest desire for each of us is for us to join Him in what He is doing. Not for us to invite Him along on our journey, but for us to see our life as it fits into what He is doing and being willing to walk alongside as a sheep would a shepherd. For me that meant giving up my dream, coaching basketball in exchange for something I never set out to do...running a food pantry.

For you it will probably look totally different. But what God can do with your life is greater than anything you could accomplish on your own.

I have experienced so much of the Father, that I have learned how small I am in respect. My new favorite verses are from Ephesians 3. It's one of Paul's prayers for the Ephesians.

For this reason I kneel before the Father, from whom every family in heaven and on earth derives its name. I pray that out of his glorious riches he may strengthen you with power through his Spirit in your inner being, so that Christ may dwell in your hearts through faith. And I pray that you, being rooted and established in love, may have power, together with all the Lord's holy people, to grasp how wide and long and high and deep is the love of Christ, and to know this love that surpasses knowledge—that you may be filled to the measure of all the fullness of God.

Now to him who is able to do immeasurably more than all we ask or imagine, according to his power that is at work within us, to him be glory in the church and in Christ Jesus throughout all generations, for ever and ever! Amen.

Ephesians 3:14-12 NIV

I love reading what Paul prayed for believers and praying that prayer for myself. I have learned that much can be accomplished when we pray the Father's will instead of our own. I am asking God to show me how to do that better. That's my goal for this year. I love this prayer. It's my favorite part of all Scripture. You see community in the first paragraph. Paul prays that they would understand the height, width, length and depth of the love of Christ, which surpasses knowledge and to be filled to the measure of all the fullness of God. What if we all prayed that prayer daily? I love that part.

But my favorite part comes in the second paragraph. He can do immeasurably more than all we ask or imagine, according to His power that is at work within us. Amen! We have seen it firsthand. He is able to do more than I could ever even dream of doing. He is able to accomplish more than I could ever even think to ask Him for. I can trust Him to do what He is able to do, or I can trust myself to do my own "pressing on." I think I will choose to trust Him and watch and see what He is able to do.

Jennifer and I started a little food pantry, food closet would probably be a more fitting name. We pressed on to make sure that kids weren't leaving school without something. But when God started moving behind it, it was different. It was immeasurably different. In three years, through House of the Harvest, God has fed over 90,000 people and counting, all "according to His power that is at work in us." He made it grow. He sent the help. He orchestrated the food, the building, the donations, the volunteers. Everything that was needed to make it what it was, He provided and continues to provide. He is bigger than all of it. But only if we believe Him to be.

I don't want an ordinary life, filled with more and more ordinary things anymore. I want to be willing to pack up my things and leave on faith like Abraham did without knowing where he was going, because God can do more with my life than I could ever imagine. I want to be willing to stand face to face with the greatest power of the world, in faith, like Moses did. I want to be willing to walk away from my heritage in complete faith, like Paul did. I want to be willing to let God work in my life because He can do immeasurably more than I can even imagine. What could He do with your life if you let Him? That's my goal today, tomorrow and ten years from now. Let Him be the shepherd. He is bigger than I can imagine.

13

Prayer, Love, Food...In That Order

When we first started House of the Harvest, Thor Erlingson (now gone to do ministry in his home country of Iceland) told Jennifer and me, "People will come and help you. The volunteers will come. You will be so shocked. But you will discover that there is a whole other ministry there for them too. They are coming because they need to be healed as much as anyone that comes to get food."

I remember having my doubts about that statement when he made it. Three years of Saturday morning food distribution has taught me that was an understatement. There is so much ministry to be done.

There are so many people that are seeking an escape, healing for something in their own lives. It really has been eye-opening to me to see and experience all that we have experienced.

In Acts 6, the apostles got together with the community of disciples and decided that they needed some deacons. They knew their primary responsibility was to their ministry in regards to the word of God, and they appointed these men to take care of other matters. I love how they recognized that the daily distribution of food was an important ministry, that needed to be taken care of; however, it wasn't how they were called to spend their time. In fact they stated, they needed to devote themselves to prayer and to the ministry of the word. And that is exactly what they did.

Perspective. Keeping the proper perspective is crucial. We knew when we started that a buggy of food was only a temporary, physical answer. There are things way more important than food. In fact, Jesus Himself, during a forty day fast, told Satan in the wilderness, "Man does not live by bread alone, but by every word that proceeds from the mouth of God" (Matthew 4:4 NASB). That statement was true then and it is still true today.

You can follow the Bible all the way back to the book of Deuteronomy. You will find it tell you that the greatest command is to "love the Lord your God with all your heart, soul, mind, and strength" (Deuteronomy 6:4 NIV). And the second greatest command is to "love your neighbor as yourself" (Leviticus 19:18 NIV). Jesus, the Messiah, the King of the world repeated these statements as the two greatest commands. In fact, He took it even a step further when He said, "On these two depend all the Law and Prophets" (Matthew 22:40 NIV).

At House of the Harvest, we believe there are no truer words than these words spoken by our Savior and recorded in our Scriptures. We believe life reinforces these statements. The only thing that can satisfy your soul is a relationship with God, your Father. There is no earthly relationship that can satisfy that longing inside the depths of your soul. There is no physical thing, not even food, that can satisfy that inside of you. There is no substitute for having a real, active, and alive relationship with your Creator, the One who gave Himself for you. There is no hope without Him.

At House of the Harvest, we also believe that human beings need relationship with one another. This need outweighs our own physical needs. I have heard poverty defined as the absence of relationship. I have to say that I agree. If you show me someone that struggles to maintain healthy relationships in their life, I will show you someone that will struggle to find happiness, peace, and joy. God created us to be in relationship with one another. Loving someone and being loved by someone fills us more than any amount of food ever could.

Our motto has become "Prayer, Love, Food...in that Order." That is what we believe. And that is what we preach. We have had people who come to get food on a regular basis tell us they come for the fellowship. One person told us, "This place is the only place that someone smiles at me all week." Another said, "Eating breakfast here is like my vacation." We have had volunteers say things like, "This place saved my life." We have seen firsthand how it has brought people out of depression, given them a purpose, healed a broken and damaged soul.

Every Saturday we echo Prayer, Love, Food. You see volunteers wearing it on the back of their House of the Harvest t-shirts. Why? Because it communicates our priorities...it tells what we believe in. We believe in relationship with God above all things. We pray before we open and it is our goal each week to offer prayer to every single individual on a personal level before they leave. We believe in what the Bible says about prayer…

- "He will respond to the prayer of the destitute; he will not despise their plea." - Psalm 102:17 NIV
- "The Lord is near to all who call on Him, to all who call on Him in truth." - Psalm 145:18 NIV
- "Do not be anxious about anything, but in every situation, by prayer and petition, with thanksgiving, present your requests to God." - Philippians 4:6 NIV
- "Pray without ceasing." - 1 Thessalonians 5:17 NIV
- "Therefore I want the men everywhere to pray, lifting up holy hands without anger or disputing." - 1 Timothy 2:8 NIV
- "Therefore confess your sins to each other and pray for each other so that you may be healed. The prayer of a righteous person is powerful and effective." - James 5:16 NIV

Scripture shows us that it was part of Jesus' normal practice to remove Himself for the purpose of prayer. He was the One who stated in Mark 11, "Therefore I tell you, whatever you ask for in prayer, believe that you have received it, and it will be yours" (Mark 11:24 NIV). Our primary goal at House of the Harvest is to use what God has blessed us with to point others toward Him. And not just to talk about God, but to show real, authentic, genuine relationships with the Father in ways that may cause people to recognize, as Jesus said, "You are the Light of the world. A city that is set on a hill cannot be hidden" (Matthew 5:14 NIV).

The Bible has a whole lot to say about love. Paul probably said it best in 1 Corinthians 13 when he said,

> "If I speak in the tongues of men or of angels, but do not have love, I am only a resounding gong or a clanging cymbal. If I have the gift of prophecy and can fathom all mysteries and all knowledge, and if I have a faith that can move mountains, but do not have love, I am nothing. If I give all I possess to the poor and give over my body to hardship that I may boast, but do not have love, I gain nothing."

> 1 Corinthians 13:1-3 NIV

Without the presence of love, there are a whole lot of things that don't matter. In the mind of Jesus, the two greatest commands began with the word love. Paul wrote to the Romans and said, "Whoever loves others has fulfilled the law" (Romans 13:8 NIV). And John wrote the following in 1 John 4:

> "Dear friends, let us love one another, for love comes from God. Everyone who loves has been born of God and knows God. Whoever does not love does not know God, because God is love. This is how God showed his love among us: He sent his one and only Son into the world that we might live through him. This is love: not that we loved God, but that he loved us and sent his Son as an atoning sacrifice for our sins. Dear friends, since God so loved us, we also ought to love one another. No one has ever seen God; but if we love one another, God lives in us and his love is made complete in us."

1 John 4:7-12 NIV

If we take a long, hard look at the life of Jesus, I think we begin to notice how well He actually did love. It is clear from His interactions. He crossed all the normal social barriers and customs. He carried Himself with so much love for others that it caused people to question Him on a regular occurrence. Why does this man eat with sinners? Why does He let that woman touch Him? Surely He doesn't know what kind of woman she is? Why does He talk to Samaritans? Why does He not shame this woman for her adultery? Why would He go to the house of a tax collector? Why? Why? Why? Everything Jesus did caused them to ask questions. The answer to all those questions is love.

He ate with them, because He loved them. He let her anoint His feet and wipe them with her hair because He loved her. He defended her and delivered her from stones because He loved her. He called him out of the tree and went to His house because He loved him. In fact, I think that Jesus would say the truest test of our spiritual growth is not in how well we know the Bible, how many worship services we attend, or even in our good deeds. The truest test of spiritual growth is in how well we love and especially how well we love those that aren't like us. In fact, the first time He spoke to a crowd, hear what He had to say...

"You have heard that it was said, 'Love your neighbor and hate your enemy.' But I tell you, love your enemies and pray for those who persecute you, that you may be children of your Father in heaven. He causes his sun to rise on the evil and the good, and sends rain on the righteous and the unrighteous. If you love those who love you, what reward will you get? Are not even the tax collectors doing that? And if you greet only your own people, what are you doing more than others? Do not even pagans do that? Be perfect, therefore, as your heavenly Father is perfect."

Matthew 5:43-48 NIV

I find it interesting that He talks about loving those who are your enemies, loving those who don't love you, those who have no reason to love you, those who aren't your own people. They don't look like you, act like you, think like you. And then, He draws a conclusion to that message by saying, "Be perfect, as your heavenly Father is perfect" (Matthew 5:48 NIV). It's as if He is saying for us to walk in perfection on this earth is to love perfectly, just as our Father did when He chose to love each of us. You may not understand them. You may not be able to relate to them. You may not even care to be around them. But you can always love them. For us to live perfectly, means to love, deeply love everyone, regardless. That's what the Father did for you. And that is exactly the message we want to send at House of the Harvest.

We know it's the food that brings people. If there is no food, there are no families at the door. If there is no food, there are no volunteers. If there is no food, there is no opportunity for ministry to be done every Saturday morning at 9144 Wall Triana Hwy. in Harvest, Alabama. But God continues to provide the food, and as long as He does, we will continue to model seeking Him with all of our being and loving everyone as perfectly as we are capable, even if they aren't like us. Prayer, Love, Food...in that order. It's what we do.

14

Two Fish

I went out to the garage early one morning to get a workout in. There were a lot of days that I would go out, spend a few minutes in prayer, or even study before my workout or even between sets. This morning was no different in that regard. But it was somewhat different. It was a Monday. And it was following a Sunday that had really challenged my thinking. Jennifer and I had been at church at our home, the Light, that Sunday morning. And, I won't go into details, but what had happened that Sunday morning put me in a place to really seek God.

How does He work in the world today? How close is He to me as a believer? Does He desire to communicate with me on a personal level? Has He not before because my faith was too small? Or had He been all along and I was crediting other things for what was really

God speaking to me? These are tough questions to explore when you first begin to really explore them. When you start to have your thinking challenged by people and events around you, it is a difficult place to be. But, for me, I would rather give God too much credit than not enough. And that is where I was this Monday morning. Wrestling with who God really is. I was raised in church. I have studied the Bible all my adult life. And now I am finding out how little I actually know about God. It's intimidating. But it put me in a place where I desired the answers and I only desired to get them from the Source.

Saul was in a similar place after his experience on the road to Damascus. Jesus had appeared to him, challenged his thinking, and sent him in a new direction. I was about to be sent in a new direction.

That Monday morning, I sat down on my weight bench in the garage, and I had a heart to heart with God from a place of total confusion in my mind. I vividly remember telling God, "I don't even know what to believe. I don't care what anyone says, I just need to know from You."

While I was praying that morning, I was completely overtaken. I don't know any other way to describe it. I felt this pressure rising from my gut all the way to my head. For a moment, it was like my head was going to explode. My eyes just filled with tears as I heard God speak to me, "I am here. I am here." Over and over and over. The next thing I knew, I was laying in the floor of my garage, overwhelmed with emotion, tears flowing that I could not contain, my head flooded with the voice of God over and over and over. It was like God was literally sitting in our garage with me.

I saw a vision of myself standing in a field, my arms were open, and all these children of different races were running to me. Little children just running to my arms. And it was like I was in the moment, thinking and feeling what was happening. I remember thinking, "What am I supposed to do?" Above me a cloud with the appearance of Jesus standing, looking down over and He spoke these words, "Just let them come."

I never did lift a weight that morning. I was so overcome in that moment. It was the answer to my prayers. Never again would I doubt that God desires a personal relationship with every one of us. Seek and you will find. Knock and the door will be opened unto you" (Matthew 7:7 NIV). Since then my relationship with God has grown tremendously. Once it begins, I don't know that anything on this earth satisfies the soul.

I am still waiting for Him to reveal all that the vision I had that day means. I am confident that I will know one day. But for now, what I know is that God has given us a mission. That mission is to make life better for the children of the world who are hopeless, broken, suffering, and rejected. I don't know what all that looks like, but we didn't know what House of the Harvest looked like either. We were just trying to get food to some children that needed it, one loaf of bread at a time. We were just bringing our two fish each day. God was handling the rest.

And He will continue to, because He is faithful. I spent a long-time asking God to be with me on my journey. I knew where I was going, how I was going to get there, and what it was going to look like when I got there. I was wrong about all of it. Now I see the joy of being like Abraham. God called me to go, so I packed my things and went. I don't know where I am going. I don't know how I am going to get there. I don't know what it is going to look like or what exactly He has in mind. But I do know this, and it allows me to walk in confidence: He has it under control and He will show me when He is ready. It is the Father who calls and the Father who sends. If I had to choose between following Him without knowing where it would lead or creating my own plan and begging Him to join me, I will choose ignorance every time. Why? Because He has already proven to me that He can do immeasurably more than all I can ask, dream, or imagine. He told me that in Ephesians 3. Then He showed me that His promise was real. The only thing that matters to me now is being on His journey. He's my Father. He's my King.

All of that brings me to today. Jennifer and I are setting out to start a new organization, Two Fish Ministries, with the mission of helping children where we are to overcome the struggles that they face in this life and doing it in Jesus' name. Our goal is simply to make life better for the children around us that need it most, because we are surrounded by them.

The name is significant. The story is of utmost relevance. It was a child that brought Jesus those two fish that day. It was a child who gave everything he had to the man he did not know. It was a child whose gift the King of the world would use to do great things.

The similarities are striking. It wasn't much that little boy brought. We don't have much to bring either. When he handed over that basket, no one there had any idea what Jesus was going to do with it. We don't know exactly how He is going to move in our lives either. But that little boy had faith enough that somehow, someway, that Man that everyone spoke of could do something with what he had. And that is the one thing we don't doubt either.

It's the story of the two fish. The two fish that changed the lives of many. Not because they had food that day, but because they met a Savior, and a King that day.

When House of the Harvest started four years ago, we always knew that it was a fingernail to what God was going to do. It was only a piece. After all, giving a family in need a little bit of food for the week only puts them in a position to return the next week. We knew this when it started. It wasn't the answer to the poverty problem in our community...it was a piece of the answer. It was a big step toward the answer. As a matter of fact, our hope was that it would open doors for people to enter relationship with God and community with each other in ways that would produce fruit in their lives.

Two Fish Ministries is a step toward being bigger than a food distribution center. It's a step toward a ministry organization that is larger than food. It's a step toward a journey of helping children in need find better lives, better futures. Four years ago, we knew they wouldn't care about school as long as they were running on empty stomachs. That hasn't changed. When you are trying to find your next meal, an education doesn't seem so important. House of the Harvest brought a solution to that problem. Now we can move forward with finding a solution to the other problems. How do we help these children find better futures? How do we help them break generational cycles? How do we instill confidence in them that they can be more than they can even dream? Two Fish Ministries as an organization is to attack a bigger problem than hunger. It is to bring transformation in the lives of suffering children in the name of Jesus. That is the journey we want to be on. The journey of transformation. That is the journey that God seeks to draw all of us into.

We ask you to join us on our journey. Pray for us to have wisdom. Pray for us to be led by the Spirit of God. Pray for us to be shown where to go, one step at a time. Pray for us to always be willing to give our two fish and trust Him with the rest. He is the One who accomplishes. Paul said it best, "I planted, Apollos watered, but God was causing the growth" (1 Corinthians 3:6 NASB). We trust that.

I pray we will always continue to do exactly what has gotten us where we are. That was meeting any need in front of us that we could in any way possible. We were just trying to put peanut butter in a cabinet and get it into the hands that needed it. James says, "If one of you says to them, 'Go in peace; keep warm and well fed,' but does nothing about their physical needs, what good is it?" (James 2:16 NIV). He calls that faith without works. We weren't interested in faith without works.

At the time, our vision was to not let any child go home hungry. God had the vision for House of the Harvest. And so began a change in our lives. A journey of faith and trust. A reliance on God, because clearly, He's got it. He can work out details in moments that would take man millennia. Believing He will, really does move mountains (Matthew 17:20 NIV).

So the lesson that we learned...don't put a ceiling on Him. Don't put walls around Him. Don't even try to define Him. Because, "you cannot understand the work of God, the Maker of all things" (Ecclesiastes 11:5 NIV).

What does the future hold? What is the vision? The vision is to let the Author do what He does. Trust Him to write the book. And we are going to do what we did from the beginning...be faithful to meet the need that is immediately before us. There are times when we can, and He honors our faithfulness. There are times when we can't, and He provides so that we can. Either way...it's humbling to be a part of.

Our passion is brokenness. Poverty. Children. And we want to walk in the middle of it. Because that is what Jesus did. He healed brokenness by going toward it, loving it, transforming it. Drawing into relationship with it. And the Holy Spirit allows us to do the same.

Our vision is to do just that. Walk with the brokenness...love it, be present with it, transform it. If that is as simple as a cup of water...we don't want anyone to be thirsty. If they are in need of food...we don't want anyone hungry. If they are sleeping on the floor...we don't want anyone without a bed. If it's education...counseling...a home...or even a family...we want to meet that need. And we believe God will use us to meet the ones we can meet, and will meet the ones we can't, Himself.

So far, God has opened doors for two food pantries and a summer academy for at-risk children. We never saw any of it coming. We just stepped in each door He opened. Yes...Solomon summed it up well, "You cannot understand the work of God, the Maker of all things" (Ecclesiastes 11:5 NIV). Our vision is to get out of the way, let the Good Shepherd lead, and be faithful to where He calls and sends. Because He is the One that can do immeasurably more.

Two Fish is a ministry. It's an opportunity to share Jesus. It's sharing the transformational power of the God who is over all through real-life experiences. It's a platform for sending forward the message of God's story through books, articles, speaking engagements, and anything else God puts before us, so that we can do the work that He calls us to do. We want to share His story because His invitation was for us, and it is for you. He is waiting for you to move in faith toward the message that God is bigger, He is alive, He is real, His ways are higher than ours, and He can do immeasurably more. Bring Him what you have and watch what He can do. He is the One who multiplies.

We want you to share our story. We want you to join us on our journey. In fact, by purchasing this book, you are making a donation to Two Fish Ministries. All author royalties from Two Fish will go to Two Fish Ministries to be used by God in the lives of real people, with real needs. We can't wait to see what He does! He is the God of immeasurably more.

Your Two Fish

It had to be one of the greatest scenes to ever unfold before human eyes. Two little fish. Five barley loaves. Five Thousand men. Historians estimate a five to one ratio of women and children to men. That's thirty thousand people. Had Jesus taken the two small fish and five loaves and made twelve baskets out of it, it would have been a miracle. Not to mention that thirty thousand people ate. Because that little boy gave what he had.

I hope this book has helped you understand more about the God of the Bible. I hope it has helped you grow in your relationship with the God who created you and desires to be close to you. I hope that it has helped you to understand that God is still writing His story. You and I are a part of that story. We are part of God's mission to redeem mankind. His book isn't finished. It's not complete. It is written to a point. But not to the end of the Father's work. As Jesus said, "My Father is always at His work, to this very day" (John 5:17 NIV).

The God of the Bible is the same yesterday, today, and forever. And He desires for each of us to join Him in His story of redeeming men. We can bring our two fish, lay them at the Master's feet, and watch as He uses them to write more of His story.

My challenge to you with this book is to bring your two fish to the God of the Bible. He is real, alive, and active. His invitation still stands, "Ask and it will be given to you; seek and you will find; knock and the door will be opened to you. For everyone who asks receives; the one who seeks finds; and to the one who knocks, the door will be opened" (Matthew 7:7-8 NIV). And to the one who brings his two fish...the Father can do immeasurably more than you can ask, dream, or imagine. Increase our faith, Lord, in the name of Jesus!

two
fish

DISCOVERING THE GOD OF

IMMEASURABLY MORE

Visit twofishministries.com for more.